iT felt Like A kiss

glimpses of art in the Mission District of San Francisco

Leena Prasad

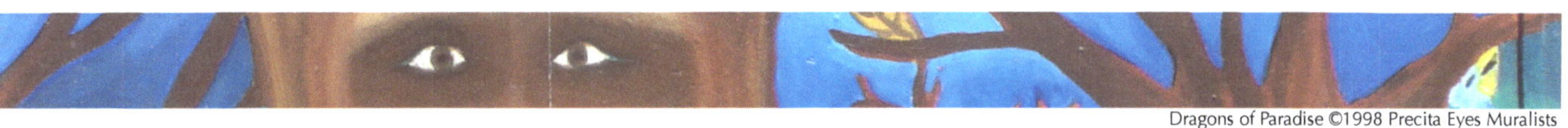
Dragons of Paradise ©1998 Precita Eyes Muralists

Thinkers Ink

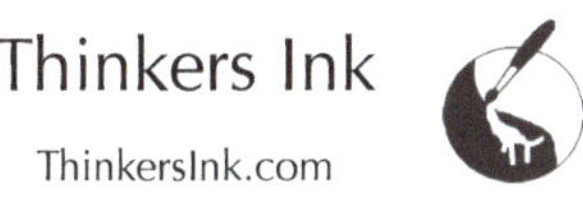

ThinkersInk.com

Originally published as a series of columns, "Visual Narratives" in the Mission Arts Monthly magazine.

This book first published in North America in 2011 by Thinkers Ink.

iT felt Like A kiss

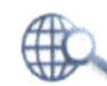 iTfeltLikeAkiss.com

 @iTfeltLikeAkiss

 iT felt Like A kiss (group)

Writer, Photographer, Design & Layout: Leena Prasad

Editor: Rebecca Rozanski

Publisher: Thinkers Ink

Thinkers Ink

P.O. Box 460271

San Francisco, CA 94146

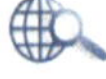 ThinkersInk.com

 @ThinkersInk

 Thinkers' Ink (group)

Printed in USA.

Library of Congress Cataloging-in-Publication Data
Prasad, Leena.
It felt like a kiss : glimpses of art in the mission district of San Francisco / by Leena Prasad -- 1st ed.
p. cm.
ISBN 978-0-9829285-0-9
1. Visual Arts -- United States 2. Visual Arts -- San Francisco, 3. Mural 4. Graffiti 5. Painting 6. Sculpture 7. Performance 8. Prasad, Leena I. Title.
2010942425

Thanks to...

Madhawi, my mom, for the artistic genes and the desire for self-expression. Dinesh, my dad, for his interest in literature and his sense of discipline for accomplishing goals. Both of you for the abundant love and support that you continuously provide.

Monica Prasad, my sister, for encouraging all my artistic endeavors and for the initial and final edits you provided for this book.

Audrey Mei for brainstorming layout and presentation of this book and for some of the edits.

Geoff Wolfe, the producer of the Mission Arts Monthly where all these articles originated.

"72% Writers" for help in shaping some of the pieces, the prologue, and the epilogue.

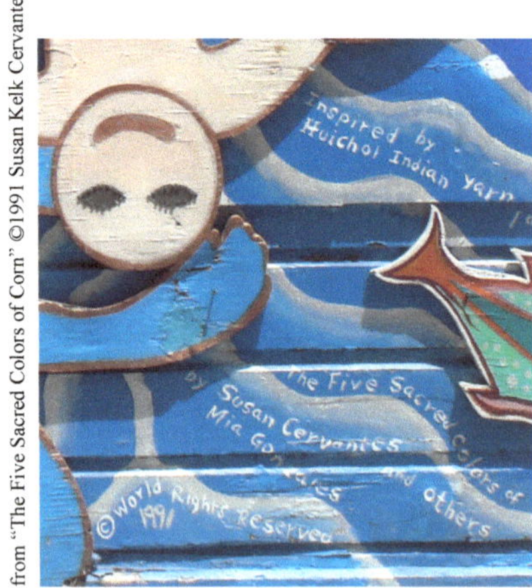

from "The Five Sacred Colors of Corn" ©1991 Susan Kelk Cervantes

dedicated to
Monica, Madhawi and Dinesh

Contents

The artist is a receptacle for emotions that come from all over the place; from the sky, from the earth, from a scrap of paper, from a passing shape, from a spider's web.

Pablo Picasso

Prologue: Visual Narratives

There's a large ear taped to the wall. It's part of a Van Gogh collage. A black and white photo cutout of his face has white gauze wrapped around the head. Red blood seeps through the bandage. By itself, this collage would be remarkable enough. Here at Radio Habana Social Club, this is one among hundreds of visual feasts awaiting your consumption. This tiny nightclub can barely fit ten, maybe twenty people. Yet the art cornucopia feels infinite.

Unexpected discoveries like this fueled my passion for writing a "Visual Narratives" column for the Mission Arts Monthly, a magazine devoted to art in the Mission neighborhood of San Francisco. I've collected all the columns in this book. There's a piece here about Radio Habana called "Visual Feast." I hope the story inspires you to visit the club and enjoy samosas and sangria along with the art. One of the owners, Leila, is always there. If her husband, the collector/curator, is around, you might even get a chance to ask him about the history of each objet d'art.

Each story in this book is a unique experience in "seeing" art with an open mind. I hope this resonates with you as you enjoy the narratives.

Leena Prasad

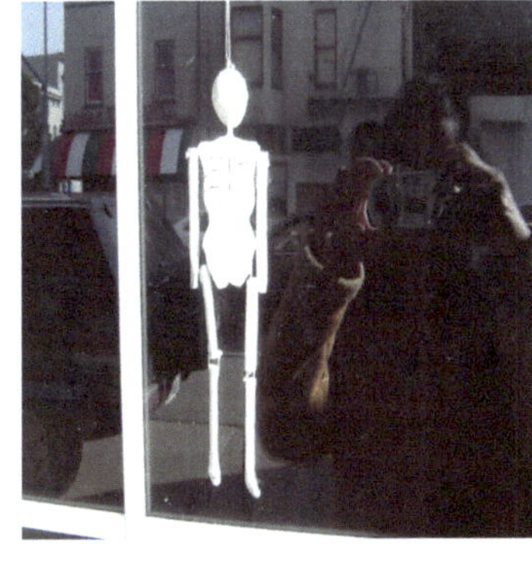

window of Radio Habana Social Club

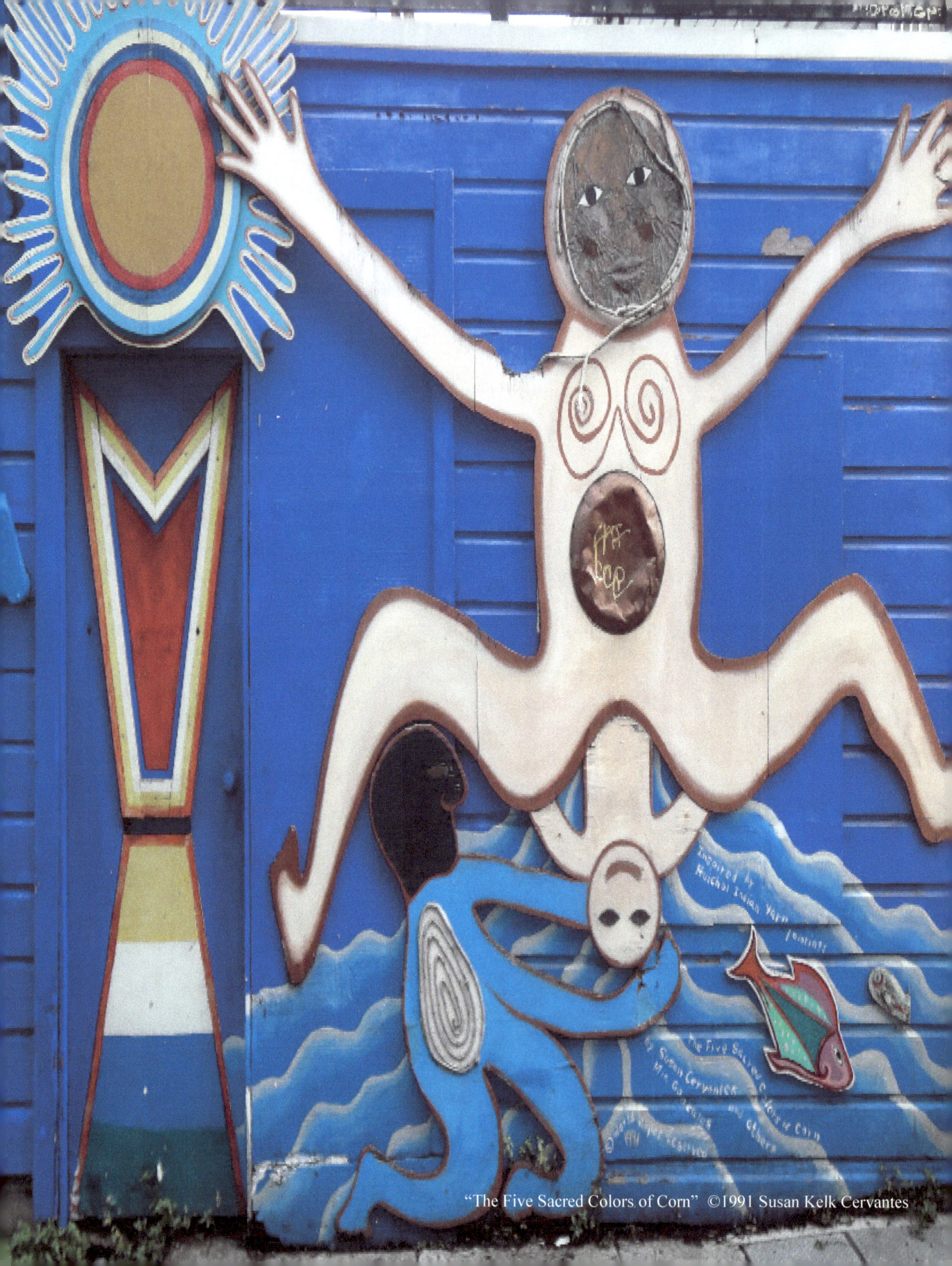

"The Five Sacred Colors of Corn" ©1991 Susan Kelk Cervantes

The Walls

Until I started living near the Mission, the murals of San Francisco were just another peripheral characteristic of this beautiful city. I knew they existed; I knew they were historical. Yet, I had very little appreciation for them. Sure, I had noticed them and had even made plans to go on a Mural Walk someday. On occasions, I took photographs of a particularly striking mural. They hadn't, however, been successful in competing for my attention against all the art museums in this city.

My attitude changed when I was looking for an ideal place to shoot a scene for a film. I wanted the location to be outdoors, near Valencia Street and someplace quiet to minimize the sound being picked up by the film microphone. Finding a good spot wasn't easy because from the overly sensitive microphone's point of view, every location was extremely noisy.

As I passed by the Elbo Room, I noticed an alley next to the nightclub. It was off Valencia, very colorful, and relatively quiet. The only negative aspect was that it was a bit dirty. That, however, was something I could handle in the filming.

The 10-15 second scene that we filmed in that alley absorbed an entire day and gave us a chance to become very familiar with the murals in Clarion Alley. As the film director and as someone who had to be the most aware of the location logistics, I walked away with a new respect for not just the aesthetic and technical appreciation of the artwork but also a new excitement for the power of art to make political statements.

At the time I had no idea that this alley near 17th Street and between Valencia and Mission Streets is quite famous. The murals painted on the walls here are planned with detailed sketches and draft paintings, proposed to a committee, and approved before anything goes on the walls. After completion of the work, a block party is organized to celebrate the piece. This practice of painting the walls of Clarion Alley started in 1992.

Now hooked on the murals, I wanted to find out more. So, I signed up for a mural tour with Precita Eyes, the governing organization and arts collaborative. They offer several mural tours every week. The tour started with a slide presentation of the murals of San Francisco. Here is where I learned that a mural is "anything" painted on a wall, contrary to my previous understanding that a mural must adhere to a specific style and political agenda.

I learned that most murals in San Francisco are narratives of Latin American politics or culture and many of them can be found on walls and alleys in the Mission. One of the slides featured Diego Rivera's self portrait where he's shown working on a mural. I recalled seeing this mural at a tour of the San Francisco Art Institute that I had attended as part of an Art History class.

After the slide presentation, we walked

down Balmy Alley where we feasted on a visual spread of colors and passions. One mural depicted political struggles of women in Latin American and other developing nations; another captured the shadows of peoples' lives in wartime El Salvador. Most of the murals displayed messages of political or religious significance. There were some, however, that were painted for pure aesthetic pleasure.

We moved on to view other murals in nearby alleys. There was one painted in monotonic blue with sprinkles of red and depicted several political scenes. One of the scenes was of people and water and the tour guide explained that it was a reference to how Bechtel Corporation of San Francisco overcharges people in developing countries for water that belongs to the people but has been quarantined by Bechtel.

At the end of the tour, I was feeling a multitude of mixed emotions. As a painter, I felt that a new world of possibilities had opened up to me. Yet, I felt frustrated with my own work which now appeared stale in comparison to the passion expressed in the murals. As an art connoisseur who had learned about visual art on a self-taught three-week long visit to Paris and follow-up visits to the South of France, I felt that I had limited myself by placing myself on a Chagall/Dali/Magritte continuum that had become a staple and a reference point for judging all paintings. As a card carrying member of the SFMoMA and several of the art museums in San Francisco, I felt cheated out of the excitement that political art can generate. Even the Diego Rivera pieces I had seen at SFMoMA and the Frida Kahlo pieces I had seen everywhere had not had the same impact on my heart as the wall art easily accessible and abundant in San Francisco.

Why?

It was only after journaling thoughts about the experience and sharing those thoughts with others that the reason for the murals' appeal became clear. In the past, the intellectual and playful contents of paintings had resonated most with me. The murals, however, reached far deeper by resonating with my political needs. They also validated my quest for finding meaning in art, a meaning beyond aesthetic pleasure.

The murals pictured here are on Balmy Street, near 24th Street, very close to the office of Precita Eyes.

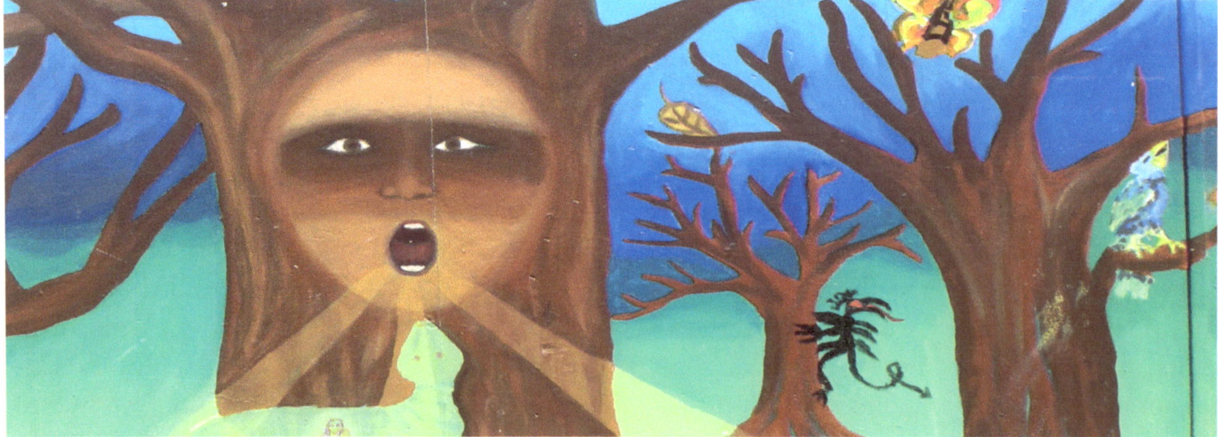

"Dragons of Paradise" ©1998 Precita Eyes Muralists

What You See / iT felt Like A kiss

"I really like this one."

"Why?"

"I don't know. But it's great."

The subject of this discussion, one of my photographs, is hanging just outside my studio. Thus, I overhear the conversation. I've sold several copies of that particular photograph. It's a simple composition: a white fire hydrant on the left, a black grill window on the right, gray sidewalk and gray walls. And the words "iT felt Like A kiss" spray painted across the wall, in bold red strokes.

The graffiti that I photographed has been whitewashed from the wall on 19th Street between Florida and Portrero Streets in The Outer Mission area of San Francisco. But, the words have dripped into my subconscious and onto the walls of my art studio and into some people's homes.

(I'm writing this column in my studio. Someone just walked in to ask if "iT felt Like A kiss" is my photograph. I love that photograph, he says. Were you the one talking about it earlier? I ask. No, I just saw it, he says).

"So, does it belong to you or the person who wrote those words?" a friend asks. "Well, I took the photograph…" I say, with a vague uncertainty creeping into my voice. The words on the wall, the colors, and the scene affected my synapses in a way that inspired me to capture it all. So, is this my art or does it belong to the person who spray painted those words? Did they plan the location, the colors, the effect? Did they also photograph their creation? I wonder if the person who wrote those words might walk into my studio one day and claim them back. How would I respond?

Earlier in the day, a woman came into my studio. "I want to show you something," she said. She took me to the photograph and said, "I have the same photo - in black and white. Would you like to trade?" After she left, the thought crossed my mind that perhaps many other people have this same photo (but not quite my composition) and where does that place mine in the art spectrum?

These are just some of the thoughts and experiences that I have at this year's October Open Studios. Only a few years ago, I was on the other side of this scene, a visitor to the studios rather than a "resident" artist. Now, I barely recall being on "the other side," tentatively looking at paintings, photographs, sculptures, mixed media… trying to connect to something, to take something home with me that would change my life in some small way… It didn't happen.

Despite the fact that I was de voted to spending at least one day of each of the four October Open Studio weekends trolling through various neighborhoods, flexing my art appreciation muscles, I never bought anything. Maybe that's why I sought out a course of study in Visual Arts, to become an artist myself, and to enhance my visual perceptions. In my art program, I drew for hours, painted for days, spent frustrating hours with messy clay, struggled with color theory, and also learned to appreciate the diverse works of my fellow artists.

With the help of my classes and with an emotional openness to my classmates' work, my taste in art matured. I started to see art differently. I graduated from a strict loyalty to only a few select painters and styles to a new appreciation for a wide variety of artists and styles. I purchased local artwork at an auction sponsored by Canvas Café. I love these newly acquired pieces but would probably not have noticed them before my self-induced art education. As if this wasn't enough of a departure from my existence as an ungenerous pseudo art aficionado, I recently embraced a non-objective (not based on any real world objects) painting style. A few years ago, I would have marginalized this style as beyond my comprehension. I enjoyed creating these pieces and I take pleasure in viewing them. They make me wonder how much more there is in this world that I haven't yet learned to "see"...

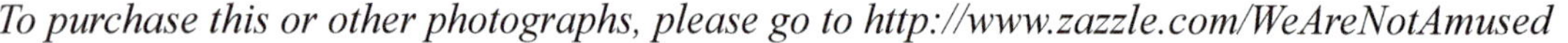
To purchase this or other photographs, please go to http://www.zazzle.com/WeAreNotAmused

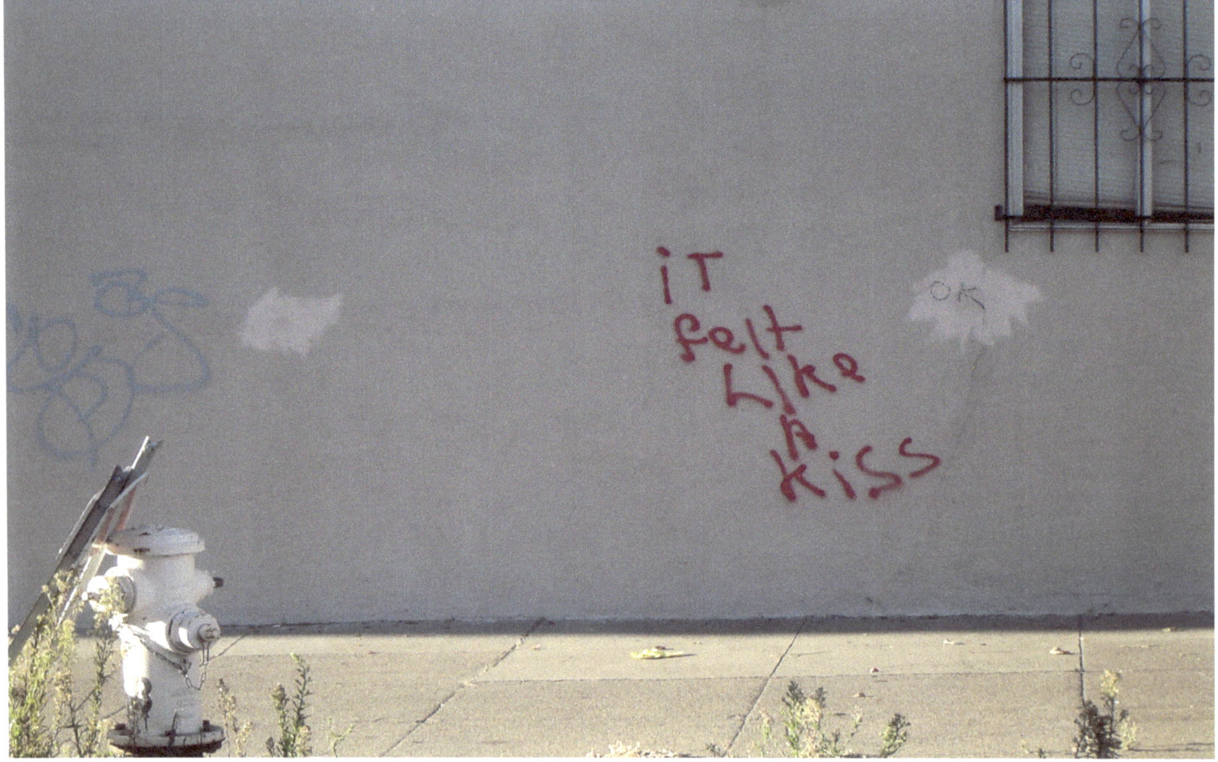

Kill Yuppys

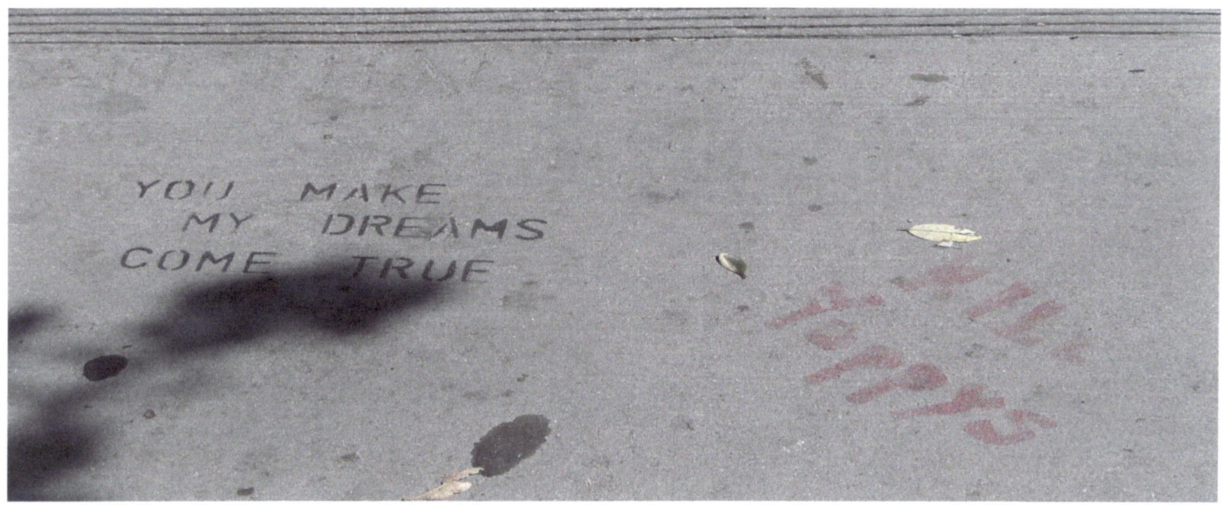

Walking along Valencia Street, I notice the words "Kill Yuppys" painted in bold red strokes on the sidewalk near 21st Street.

A stream of thoughts rush through my head. The spelling is incorrect. My profession technically qualifies me as a "yuppie." Furthermore, many of my family and friends are "yuppies."

Perhaps the words were meant to be a joke. No, I've lived in this neighborhood long enough to understand that there might be real emotions behind these words.

The sentiment prompts me to consider the court case where I had served as a juror. It was a criminal case where a passionate young defense attorney was advocating for a homeless man charged with battery on a police officer. The officer woke up the man, asleep on the sidewalk, and tried to arrest him for previous warrants for "sleeping in the park" and for being in possession of "an open container" of alcohol. The man didn't understand what was going on and resisted arrest and was charged with battery. It occurs to me that if the graffiti artist responsible for these hateful words was arrested for defamation of public property, there was a good chance that the same defense attorney, a "yuppie" might be defending this violently inclined "artist". I also realized that the jurors that I had worked with, myself included, were probably likely to support the graffiti artist's freedom of speech.

I respect a person's right to live the life they want. I tolerate the homeless who lash out insults and tell me to go back to where I came from when I don't give them money (I'm an American of South Asian descent). I respect the rights of an artist to express their opinion. In fact, I take pleasure in the graffiti on the walls, sidewalks, and bathrooms of San Francisco. I respect the voices and lives of others and I expect the same respect and tolerance for my lifestyle choices - being a yuppie is not a crime.

As I walk on, I'm unable to forget the *Kill Yuppys* stencil. Why do people see others with the lens of us vs. them, even in an area and a city where diversity is the status quo? An artist should know better. Was the person who painted those hateful words really an artist or just a mean-spirited unenlightened lost soul?

I'm bothered by these

words not only because one person (who can't spell) decided to express their opinion but also because I find this type of stereotyping prevalent among many San Franciscans. For example, some of my friends who live in the Mission consider themselves intellectually superior to people who live in the Marina. They also assume that everyone who lives in the Marina is wealthy and shallow. Some of my friends in the Marina look at the Mission as an unsafe but hip place "to visit" for its trendy restaurants and bars. My Marina friends have some concept of the artistic energy in the Mission but very few bother to venture outside the cozy confines of the expensive bars and restaurants to the dozens of small art galleries and playhouses sprinkled throughout the Mission.

Outside of San Francisco, I find that people with lazy conversation skills often resort to the clichéd practice of asking about my profession when they first meet me. It also helps to conveniently classify me before continuing with the conversation. Here, however, they ask where I live in an attempt to place me into a neatly labeled box. My response varies. Sometimes I live in the Mission, sometimes in Noe Valley, and sometimes in The Castro. Geographically, I live on the edge of all three, so I'm free to choose. I'm amused by people's responses when they hear my answer. "Noe" provokes thoughts of home, children, pets. "Mission" provokes a variety of responses ranging from the safety of the neighborhood to comments about the restaurants/bar/cafes, albeit rarely, conversations about the countless galleries or playhouses. "The Castro" causes people to look pensive. Of course it makes sense to segue into a conversation about a neighborhood after asking someone where they live. It's the tone of the conversation, the note of identification or distance, and the resulting interest or disinterest that catches my attention. It's hard to believe that I can shape a person's first impression of me based simply on which answer I select.

It's one thing to be judged by someone who lives someplace different from me. To find oppressive messages of intolerance in my own neighborhood, however, is disconcerting. During the week, my clothing is "business casual" because my job requires it. Sometimes I go to my painting studio in those clothes and protect them with a large paint-splattered man's shirt. In those moments, I'm in a different place from my computer saturated daytime world but I'm not a different person. My suit or my paint splattered shirt doesn't change who I am.

What kind of person would judge me based solely on the cut of my pants or my job rather than who I am? And not just judge, but want me to cease and desist because I happen to be different from them? Certainly, an authentic artist cannot be that limited in the scope of their imagination!

I realize that my response to the art is self-defensive. It's one of many possible reactions. I ask you to go beyond my opinion and consider other possible interpretations.

These hateful messages have mostly faded away from the sidewalks since I wrote this article a few years ago.

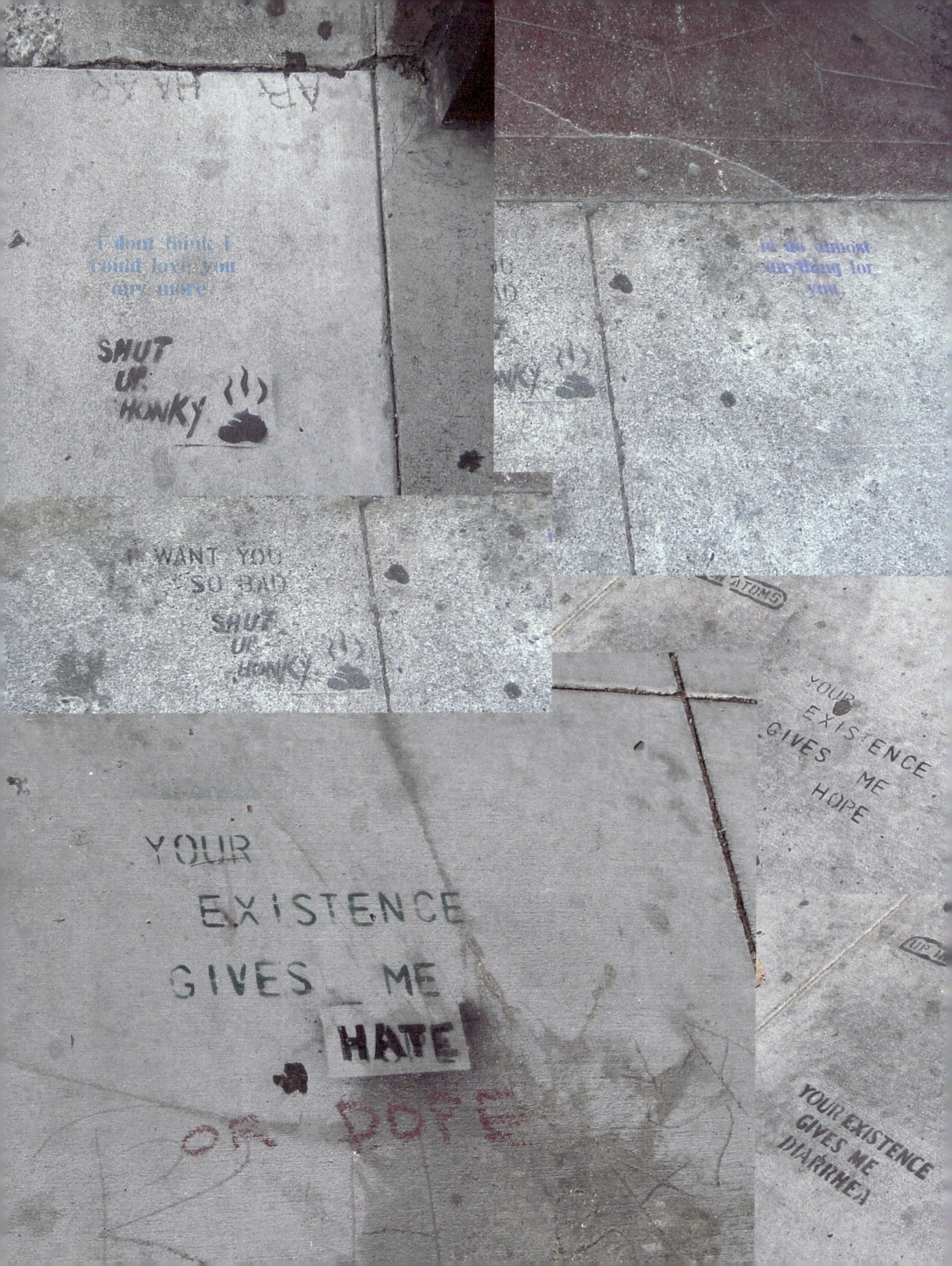

I dont think I
could love you
any more.

SHUT
UP
HONKY

id do almost
anything for
you.

I WANT YOU
SO BAD

SHUT
UP
HONKY

YOUR
EXISTENCE
GIVES ME
HOPE

YOUR
EXISTENCE
GIVES ME
HATE

OR DOPE

YOUR EXISTENCE
GIVES ME
DIARRHEA

Shut Up Honky

Your Existence Gives Me Hope, a sidewalk stencil proclaims. I pull out my tiny digital camera and snap a quick shot, happy to add another entry to my growing visual journal of the phrases stenciled into the sidewalks of the Mission. A few weeks later I notice a similar stamp, except with an update. Near the *Your Existence Gives Me Hope* is also stamped *Your Existence Gives me Diarrhea*. Although I enjoyed the sentimentality of the original graffiti, I am delighted to see that the clichéd stencil has been retrofitted into the Mission culture.

After writing the column about the *Kill Yuppys* sidewalk graffiti, I noticed an exponential increase in these pavement graffiti and an antagonistic conversation that had started between the original artist and some of the graffiti audience. A quick search on Google reveals a wide fascination with these sidewalk stencils: photos posted on Flickr.com, Webshots.com, Tribe.net, and many other websites.

Who is behind these sidewalk musings? I met a documentary filmmaker who wants to find and interview the artist. On the social network tribe.net, some people think that the messages are from a Christian group spreading its gospels. There is an ongoing debate whether these are art, vandalism, or public service. I'm not interested in knowing the artist or the culprit or the religious fanatic. The stencils have simply added a new dimension to my regular walks. Whenever I see the ubiquitous *I Want You So Bad* or *You Make My Dreams Come True* or any of the other original stencils followed by an editorial *Shut Up Honky*, I feel an affirmation of the character of the Mission. It's a place with a personality that I love more than any other neighborhood in San Francisco. I love finding a stamp that I have not seen before or a response to existing ones. I especially enjoy the new stencils' attempts to wrestle back the Mission voice from the original mushy gushy potentially religious messages that are out of tune with the "rebel with a cause" Mission culture. This "conversation" is akin to experiencing a discussion between two friends, where each side is fully committed to their own point of view.

I'm sure that not everyone is as enthusiastically supportive of these minor forms of entertainment as I am and might look upon them as nothing more than vandalism. During a recent walk, I looked around the graffiti to note if they were destroying the ambience of their surroundings. The effect was actually quite the opposite. They distract from some of the old, worn out and sometimes dirty sidewalks. I don't see these stencils in my own Noe Valley neighborhood where flowers and plants abound on the sidewalk and where these stamps would probably be washed out immediately if they were ever to make an appearance. I think they would add a delightful character to the immaculately clean Noe Valley.

To anyone who dislikes the stencils, I'd say "just walk over it." The objective of art is to stir emotions, to force people out of their everyday existence and to think beyond their world. These stenciled stamps have managed to do that by creating a dialogue.

There is also a case to be made for these as a valid genesis of art. Artists like Keith Haring whose works now hang in major museums, got their start via graffiti art. The tradition of mural paintings, which started as unsanctioned painting of public walls with traditional Mexican themes, has become a publicly funded San Francisco tradition. If those voices had been turned off, we would have missed some of the core influences on many modern visual artists and been stuck with the tired centuries old art that does not speak to the new generations or to people whose ancestry is not rooted in European traditions.

I hope these stencils, either earnest or angry, cheer up some people. I'm certainly entertained by the sarcastic responses and would be happy to support their existence with my tax dollars.

More stencils' photos at http://shutuphonky.blogspot.com

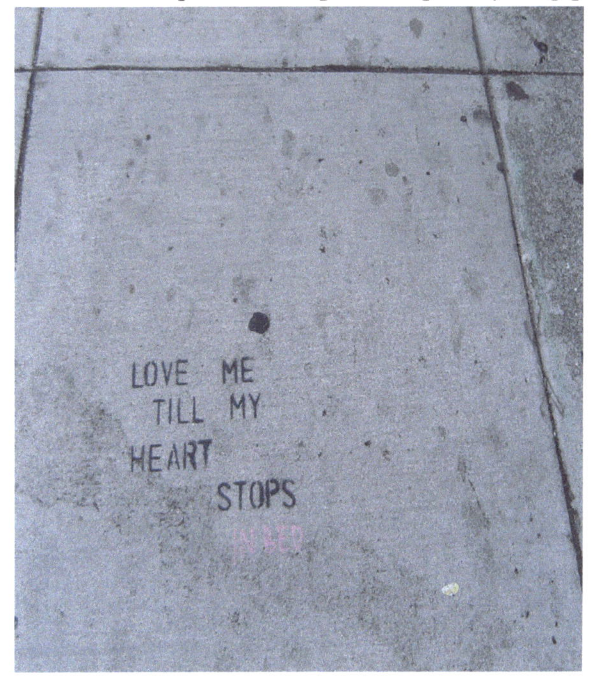

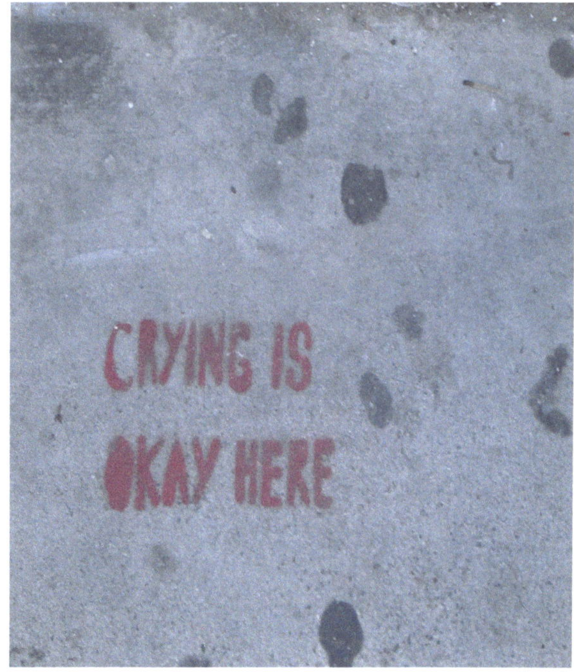

Dramatic Potentials

A man on stage tells the story of his prayers in which he begs God to not let him fail 6th grade. God disagrees with his request and tells him he must suffer the consequences of his actions. Although he fails 6th grade, he gets a kiss from a beautiful girl on the same day that he brings his report card to his father. He thanks God for the small favor.

This scene occurs in a monologue during the amateur night show by students of the ten-week performance art class at The Marsh on Valencia Street in the Mission.

The next soliloquy is by my friend Sameer. He tells the audience that his father once listed "histrionics" as one of Sameer's skills in a school admissions application. He continues to entertain us with a soliloquy about the history of his development as a theatrical artist and his current struggles against being labeled "Americanized." As a first-generation immigrant from India, he strives to maintain his identity while participating in all that America and San Francisco have to offer. His calculated exaggerations of real life events pay off in tumultuous audience laughter.

Another actor talks about her childhood in a household where all-work-and-no-play was the motto. Fortunately, she was rescued by one of her neighbors, a rich spoiled girl who introduced our protagonist to the "glamour" of smoking cigarettes and titillated her imagination with tales of sexual conquests.

Solo acts like these, often based on personal stories and contrived to elicit laughter or tears or both at the same time, are the trademark of The Marsh. The shows are successful enough to sustain the existence of this small alternative theatre. I walked away from that night's show wondering why personal stories are so compelling.

Why did a memoir like "A Heartbreaking Work of Staggering Genius" catapult the writer Dave Eggers to an acclaim that's not enjoyed by writers who create stories from their imagination? Was it for the same reason that reality television has become so ubiquitous worldwide? Does humankind harbor an insatiable curiosity for the lives of others? Or, maybe real life stories access the same "Peeping Tom" mentality invoked by indulgence in gossip.

Romans a clef, a fictional account of the lives of famous people, have enjoyed popular success over the years. Now, even the lives of ordinary people are fair game. Although the MTV show "The Real World" pioneered the idea of reality shows in the USA, the concept is not new. To my knowledge, it goes back to at least as far back as 1921 when Italian playwright Luigi Pirandello wrote a play called "Six Characters in Search of an Author."

In Pirandello's play, a real family invades the set of a theatrical rehearsal and insists that the director switch the story that the actors are rehearsing to that of the story of the family. At the time of its release "Six Characters in Search of an Author" was considered ground-breaking in its theory that real people's lives are much more interesting than the lives of fictional characters and that actors can only fake emotions whereas real people display genuine feelings.

Reality television, however, hasn't been able to find a firm foothold as a substantive mode of entertainment. Eggers's "memoirs" were "based on truth" not necessarily the exact truth. The same holds true for James Joyce who pioneered the genre of "autobiography as art" with his Portrait of the Artist as a Young Man. The solo acts at The Marsh are based on real stories but are dramatized to elicit audience emotions.

Perhaps the lives of real people will always be fodder for mass entertainment but a little bit of fine-tuning of real life, by expert hands, has the potential to achieve artistic aplomb.

"To grasp the full significance of life is the actor's duty, to interpret it is his problem, and to express it his dedication."

James Dean

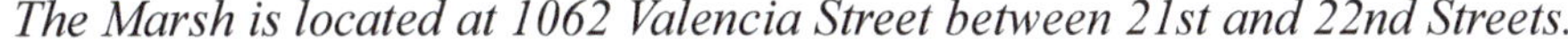

The Marsh is located at 1062 Valencia Street between 21st and 22nd Streets.

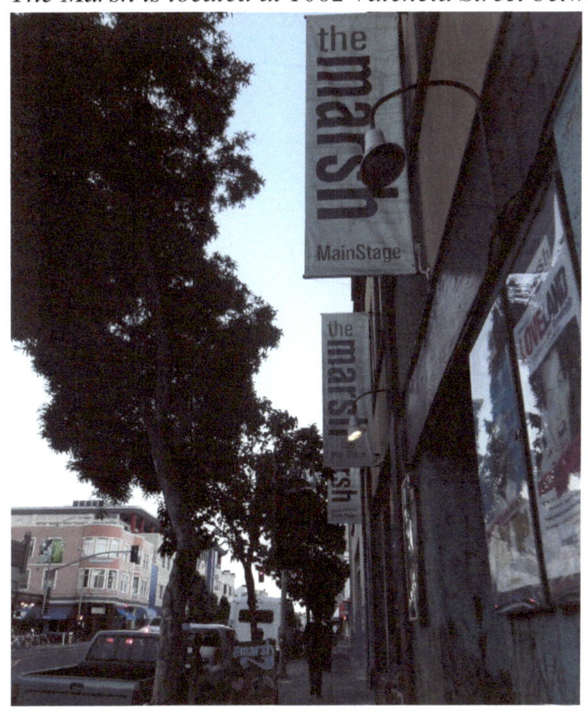

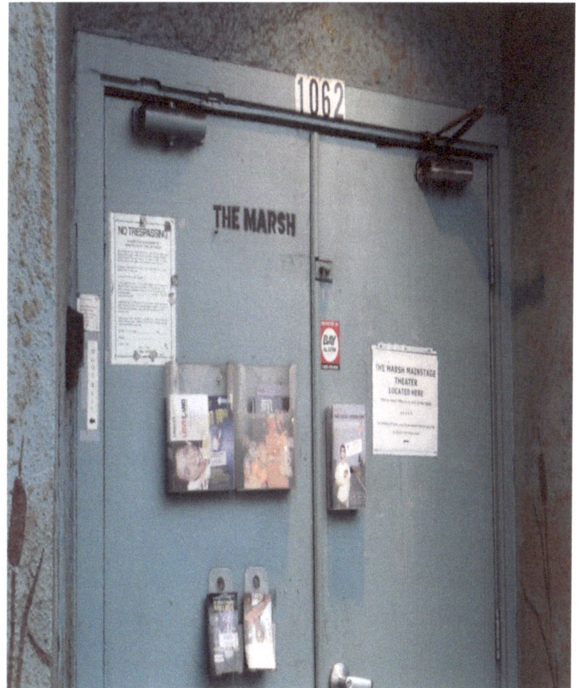

In My Own Image

A jacket and a handful of packing peanuts compete for the affections of a red wrapping paper. This isn't a surrealist plot but a puppet show, "The Wrapping Paper Caper" at The Marsh. The three main characters of the "Caper" are a Humphrey Bogart inspired detective inhabiting a jacket, a PeanutMan "bad-guy" made from Styrofoam packing peanuts, and a sexy "dame" improvised from red wrapping paper and a gold leaf garland.

Kids chuckle. Adults laugh. I wonder what is it about puppetry that delights us so? In my search for answers, I have a conversation with the crew of Lunatique Fantastique, the group responsible for the "Caper." They recount instances where audience members cried at the death of a puppet in shows exploring themes ranging from territorial warfare to WW II Japanese internment camps.

Puppets are able to tap into our emotions despite being contrived from "found objects." "No object is safe," said Slater Penney, one of the Lunatique Fantastique "Manipulators" (also known as "Puppeteers") when it comes to infusing lifelike qualities into otherwise uncharismatic objects. It usually takes at least three manipulators to handle one Lunatique Fantastique puppet: one person for the head area, one for the hands and upper body, and another for the legs and lower body. Manipulators are covered in black from head to toe so as to remain "hidden" and allow the puppets to take the center stage.

Although Lunatique Fantastique has developed a unique puppetry style and unique exploration of themes through it, the art of puppetry has existed for thousands of years. While there is no definitive history of its origins, puppetry seems to be a universal practice. I found references tracing back to masks used by primitive cultures, to the puppets found in Egyptian tombs, and to references made by Aristotle and Archimedes.

In today's digital age, new forms of this ancient art have been invented. For example, Electronics Arts' SIMS is an artificial world of people who are manipulated by users through a set of commands. In Linden Lab's Second Life, users create an avatar of themselves that can love, work, dance, fly, play, and more in a digital universe.

According to the American Heritage Dictionary, a puppet is:

1. A small figure of a person or animal, having a cloth body and hollow head, designed to be fitted over and manipulated by the hand.
2. A figure having jointed parts animated from above by strings or wires; a marionette.
3. A toy representing a human figure; a doll.
4. One whose behavior is determined

by the will of others.

That last definition reminds me of an episode of the Twilight Zone television show. A ventriloquist's dummy takes on a life of its own, pushes the ventriloquist to the edge of insanity and finally switches place with the ventriloquist.

When I was eight years old, I played the role of a puppet in a small community theatre play. Whenever my strings were pulled, I cried. Although the play was a resounding success and I became famous for my ability to cry-on-demand, my role was rather uninspiring and something I'd be loathe to repeat. I wonder if this is how a puppet would feel if a puppet could ever feel.

The Marsh is located at 1062 Valencia Street between 21st and 22nd Streets.

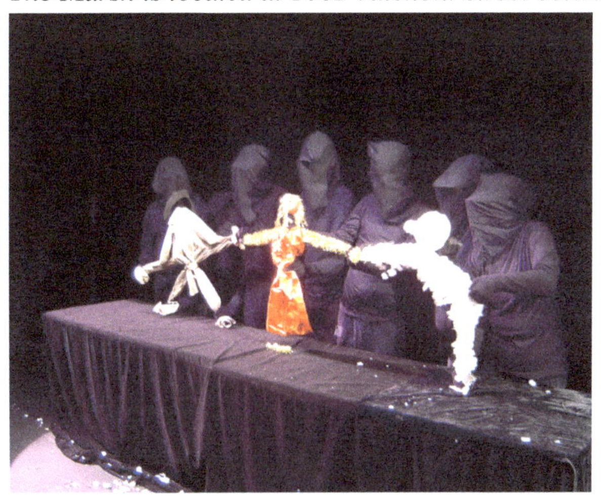

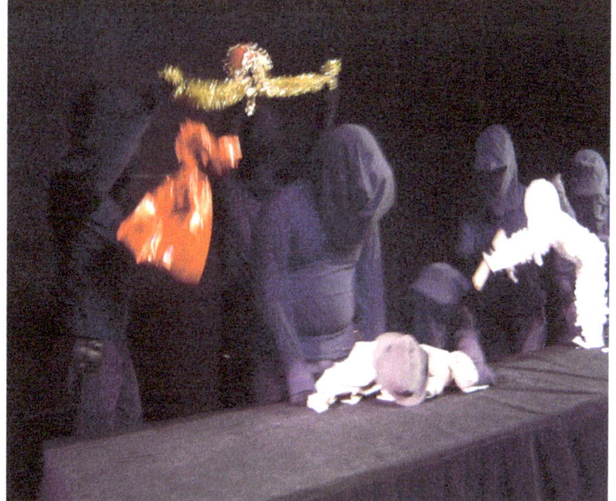

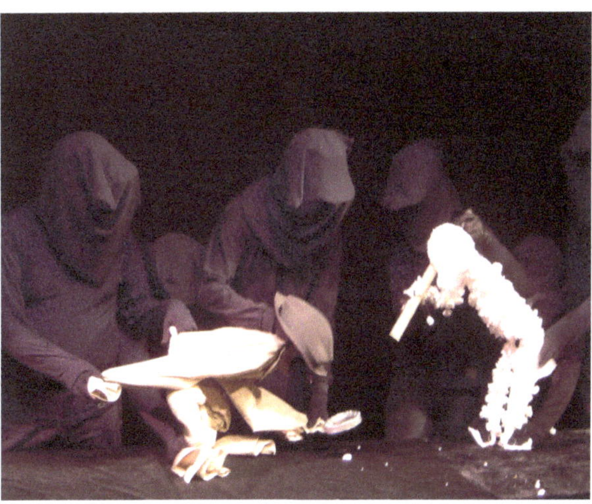

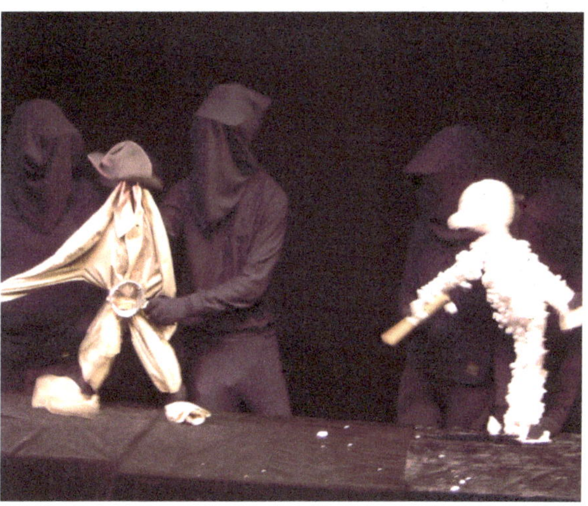

Jordan - in the Mission

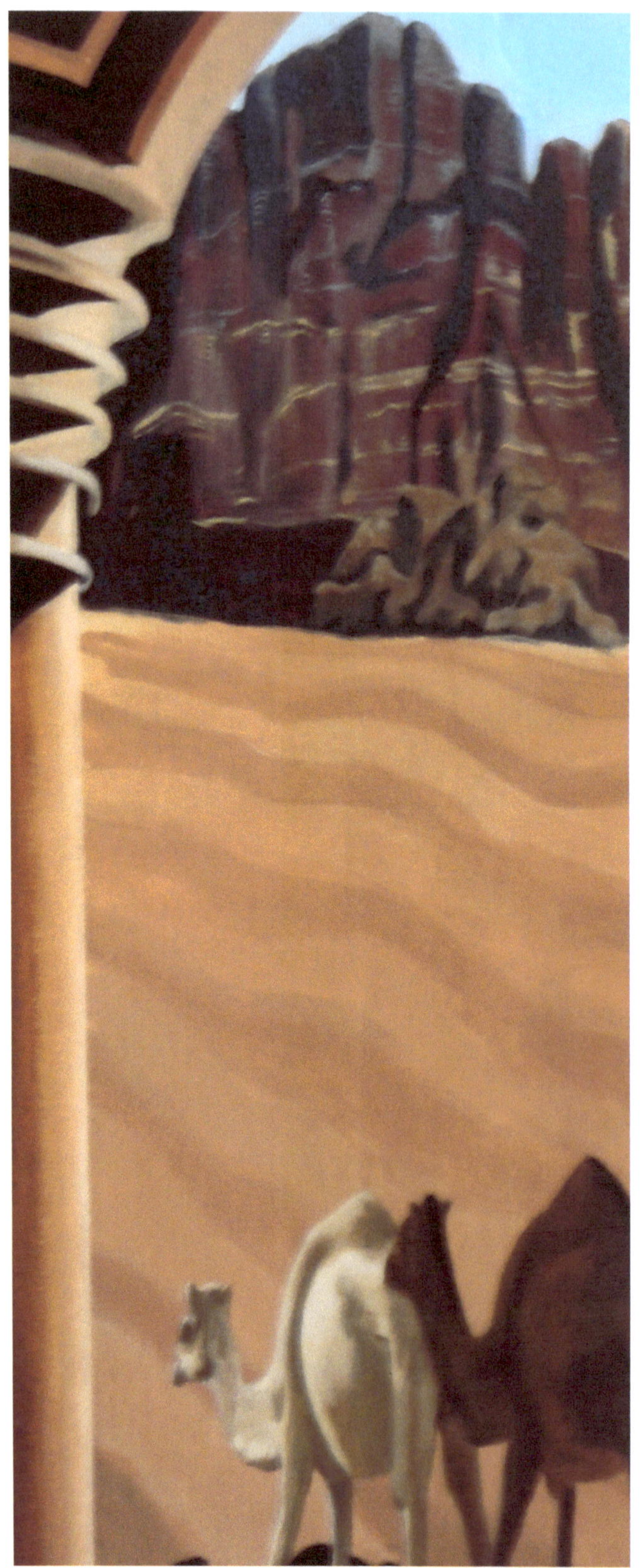

It's not that I didn't notice the murals in the café. It's just that I'm at Café Petra so often the murals became backdrops.

I was there once on a weekday when the place was not as packed as it is on the weekends. That's when I noticed the stark differences between the murals on the two sides of the inside walls. The mural on the north side is a depiction of the café's namesake, an archaeological site in Jordan called Petra. On the south are portraits of people and animals captured at slices of moments in their daily lives.

The painting on the north side is a warm kaleidoscope of oranges and reds and yellows punctuated by the blues of the sky. The building and the rocks in the mural capture the color palettes of the Petra site. The style is curvy and sensuous, seducing the viewer with the overwhelming beauty of not only the subject but that of the mural itself. Whenever I look at it, I feel transported out of the Mission and into the exotic charms of the Middle East. There is a man who stands in the mural gazing at the view. He is minuscule in comparison to the rock landscape. I try to imagine the sense of awe that I would feel if I were to go to Petra and stand in the same place.

On the south wall, shades of green and brown capture the personal daily landscapes of the people who live or lived in Jordan. On closer inspection, I notice that the paintings are partially rendered using the pointillism style.

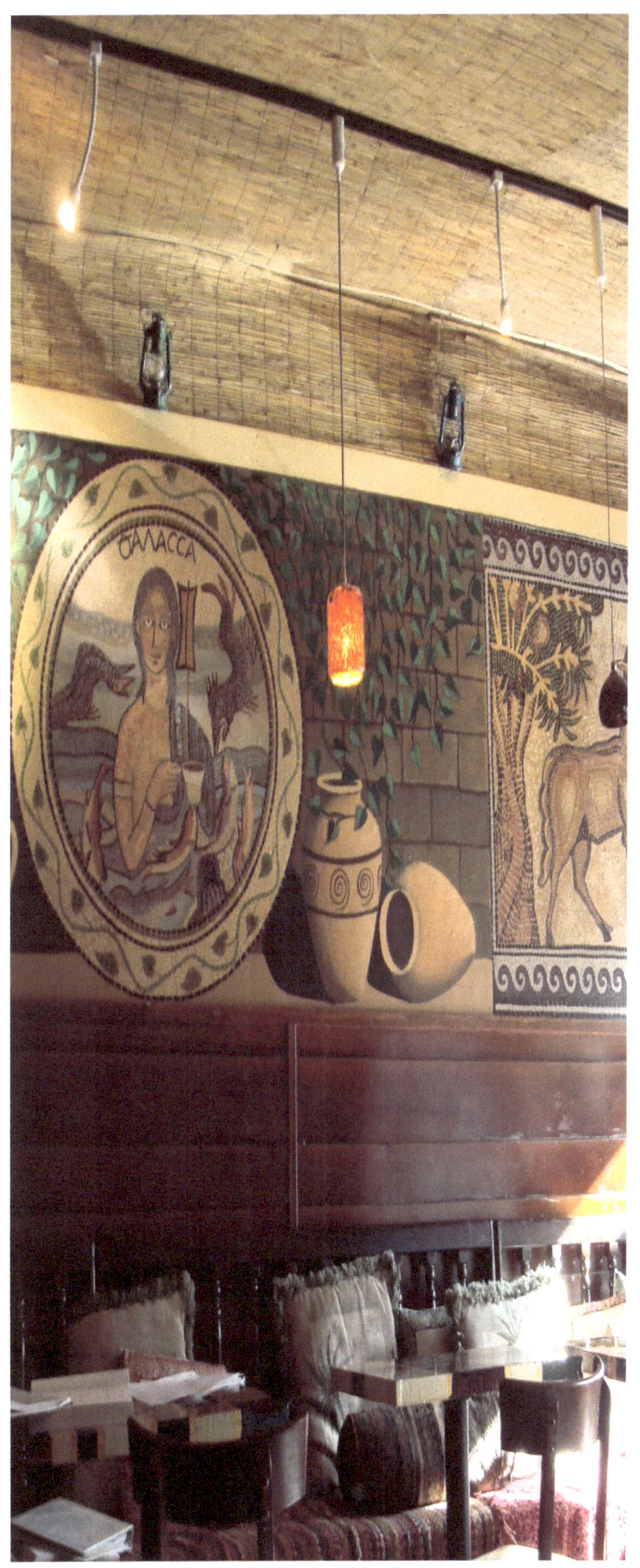

The landscape forms a realistic background into which the pointillism style portraits are "inserted." Vines with small green leaves float down over a brown brick wall covering it from the top to bottom. Terra-cotta water jugs are lined up near the wall. There are three independent portraits: two little girls, a woman, and a deer. Two of the portraits are drawn inside a "frame" and each frame is drawn as if it is hanging on the wall. The third portrait is painted on what looks like a rug hanging on the wall. The two little girls smile out at us as they stop in their play to pose - the girl in front carries the other one on her back in a piggyback ride. What have they being doing until now and what will they do afterwards? In the second portrait, a woman, perhaps a mermaid, is submerged in water, and is surrounded by fish; in her hand is a mug of coffee. The third portrait shows a deer caught in mid-run with his right front paw up in the air.

Having looked at the murals in detail for this article, I've become much more aware of the ambience they help create inside Café Petra. I often find myself gawking at the Petra mural and re-arranging the name Jordan on my priority list of places to visit. The opposing mural, with its palette of green and brown create a vision of olive trees and desert. It also offers a glimpse into the lives of the people who live love and laugh there in Jordan as I sit in the café sometime with the people with whom I live love and laugh.

I look at these murals and think about how art can transport, connect, and open up our world...even as we sit eating a bagel and sipping a coffee in a neighborhood café.

Café Petra is located at 483 Guerrero Street between 16th and 17th Streets.

Digital Murals

What's the point? This is the first thought that springs to mind when I hear about the Digital Murals project. The power of the murals in the Mission isn't contained in just their political message but also in their location and traditional style.

I consider the fact that if the murals were replaced someday by dull walls, we'd at least have the digital versions. Thankfully, given how San Francisco feels about its mural art, I feel fairly comfortable assuming that our murals will be protected past my lifetime and into the lives of future generations. So... then...why digital murals? With this question in mind, I set out to explore the twenty three murals making up the Digital Mural project.

At the website, the mural "The Mission Y2K: A History of Displacement" is a visual question of the implications of gentrification. This question is posed to both the dislocated and the dislocators. At the time of the mural's creation, the exodus of the Mission population was caused by the influx of the dot.com generation, many of whom, ironically, were digital artists. Another mural, "Ese, Last of His Tribe" approaches this same socioeconomic and cultural issue with a humorous depiction of a front-page newspaper article on Ese, "the last surviving Mexican found in the Mission district."

In another mural, "Heaven," the artist uses two panels to depict the story of a lesbian woman. The woman in the mural reinterprets her cultural influences of religion and mythology to tell her own story of being directed by an angel towards her future lover. This mural uses painting and collage techniques to tell the story in vivid details, a style that is rooted in traditional Mexican mural arts.

In "Justice is in the Eye of the Beholder," the artists trace the history of racial profiling in America by filling up most of the "wall" space with dark sunglasses that are surrounded by graphic icons. The sunglasses reflect images of the various people affected by racial profiling. The icons depict a history of racial profiling: 1882 Chinese Exclusion Act, Japanese internment camps, and the deportation of unwanted Mexican migrant farm workers.

In "Run Bush Run," George Bush tries to run away from his own nose which has grown so long that it's chasing him, threateningly close to catching up to him. This mural's editorial cartoon style leaves no ambiguity in its political message.

And lastly, "A Tribute to César Chávez" repeats the quote "The first principle of non-violent action is that of non-cooperation with everything humiliating." The quote is attributed to César Chávez which I thought was a mistake. I was sure it was a quote by Mahatma Gandhi. A quick Google search left the source unclear because some sources attribute the quote to Chávez and others to Gandhi. Whichever the case might be, this mural demonstrates one of the benefits of a digital mural over a traditional one, i.e., the attribution can be changed if it turns out to be incorrect.

There were many other murals at the website but I selected a representative set for this discussion. The murals that were created at an earlier date, held a close resemblance to the traditional murals in their expansive and painterly style. The mural styles expanded over the years to incorporate photos and cartoons and other forms of visual art. The intent of the murals, however, has stayed consistent with the traditional purposes of exploring political and social messages. All the murals continue to explore political subjects ranging from gentrification, the history of the Latin community, gay and lesbian relationships, modern politics, racial profiling, and more.

Why digital murals? After looking at these murals, my answer is why not? They are simply another medium for artistic explorations and they have the power to reach and inspire people beyond the physical borders of San Francisco. For example, I am viewing and writing this column from a hotel in Kansas City. Even though I am not in San Francisco right now, I am still able to experience the power of its political culture and art.

The murals are exhibited on the walls of Galería de la Raza during specific time periods. Details can be found at the website www.galeriadelaraza.org/eng/programs/murals.html

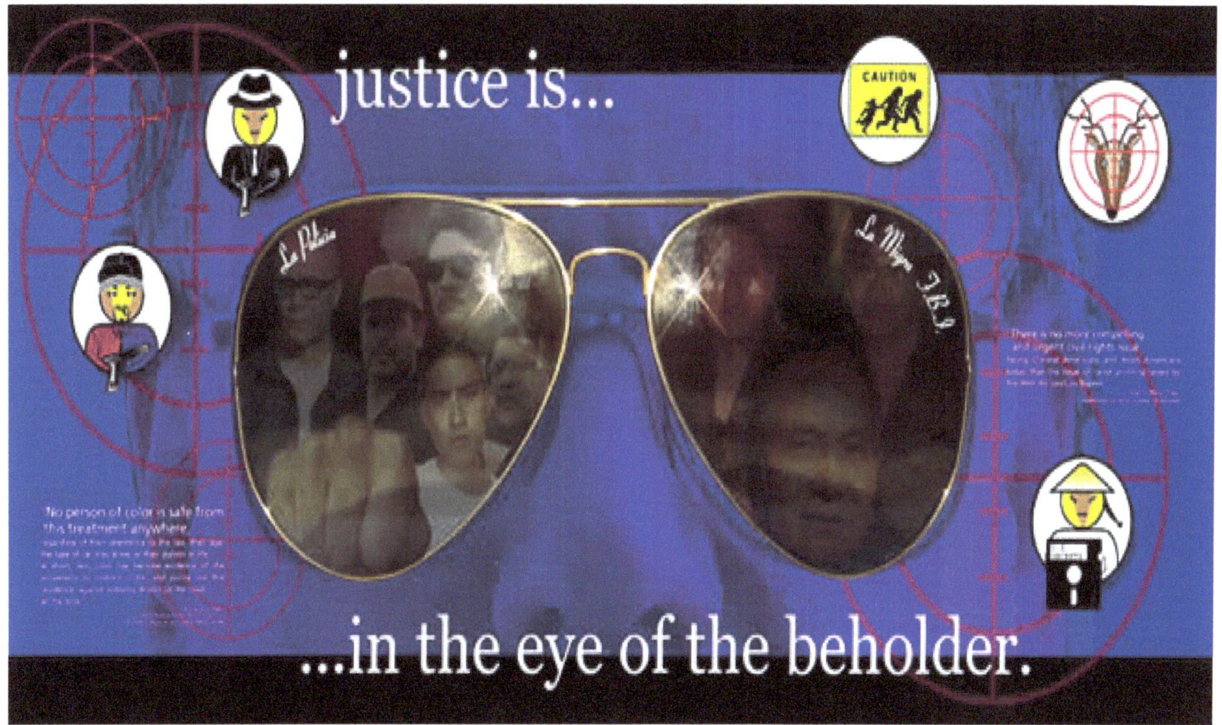

Murals Today, Gone Tomorrow

A colorful and dramatic sight captivates me as I walk around in my neighborhood. There are wood construction walkways spanning the length of 22nd Street, mid-way from Valencia Street, just past the tapas bar Esperpentos, to around the corner and across from Revolution Cafe. The walls of the temporary walkways are covered with vivid murals. I don't know how long the murals will be here so I pull out my camera and start clicking.

I usually use words to express my thoughts and impressions of the visual narratives that I find in the Mission. These images are so powerful that I'm allowing the visuals to speak for themselves.

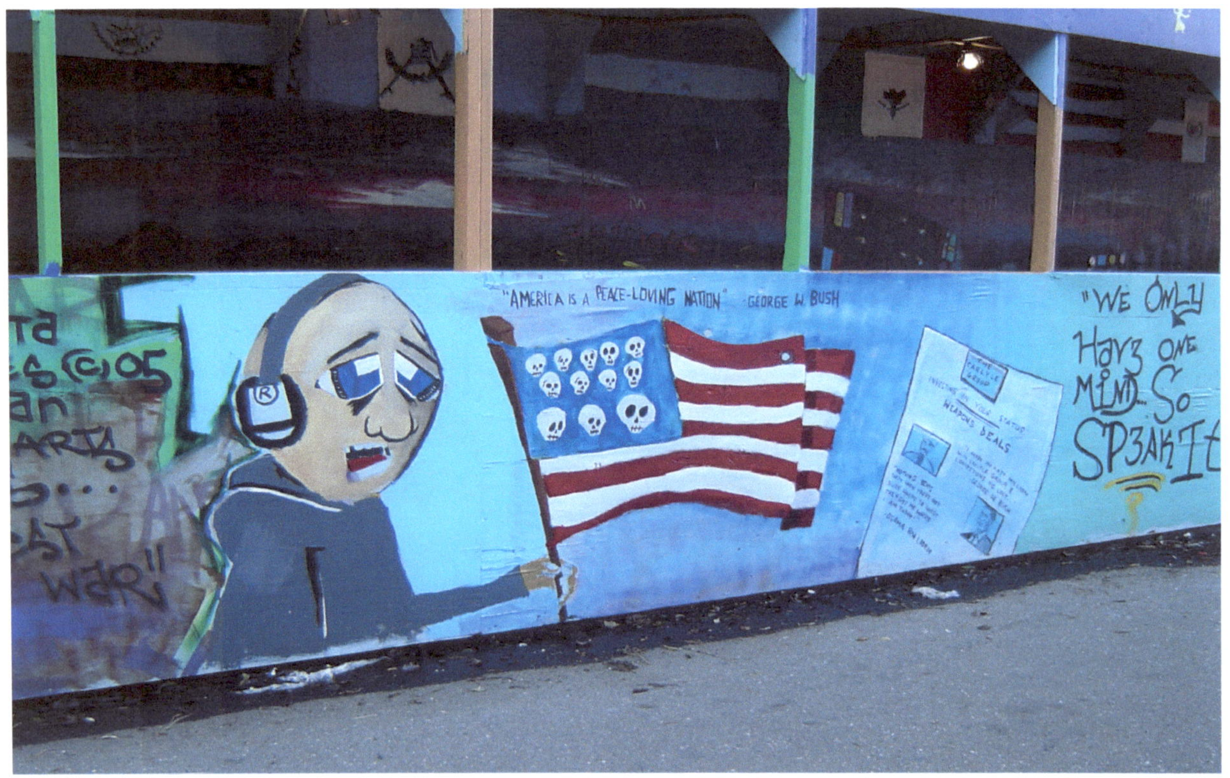

"America Is A Peace-Loving Nation" ©2005 Precita Eyes Muralists

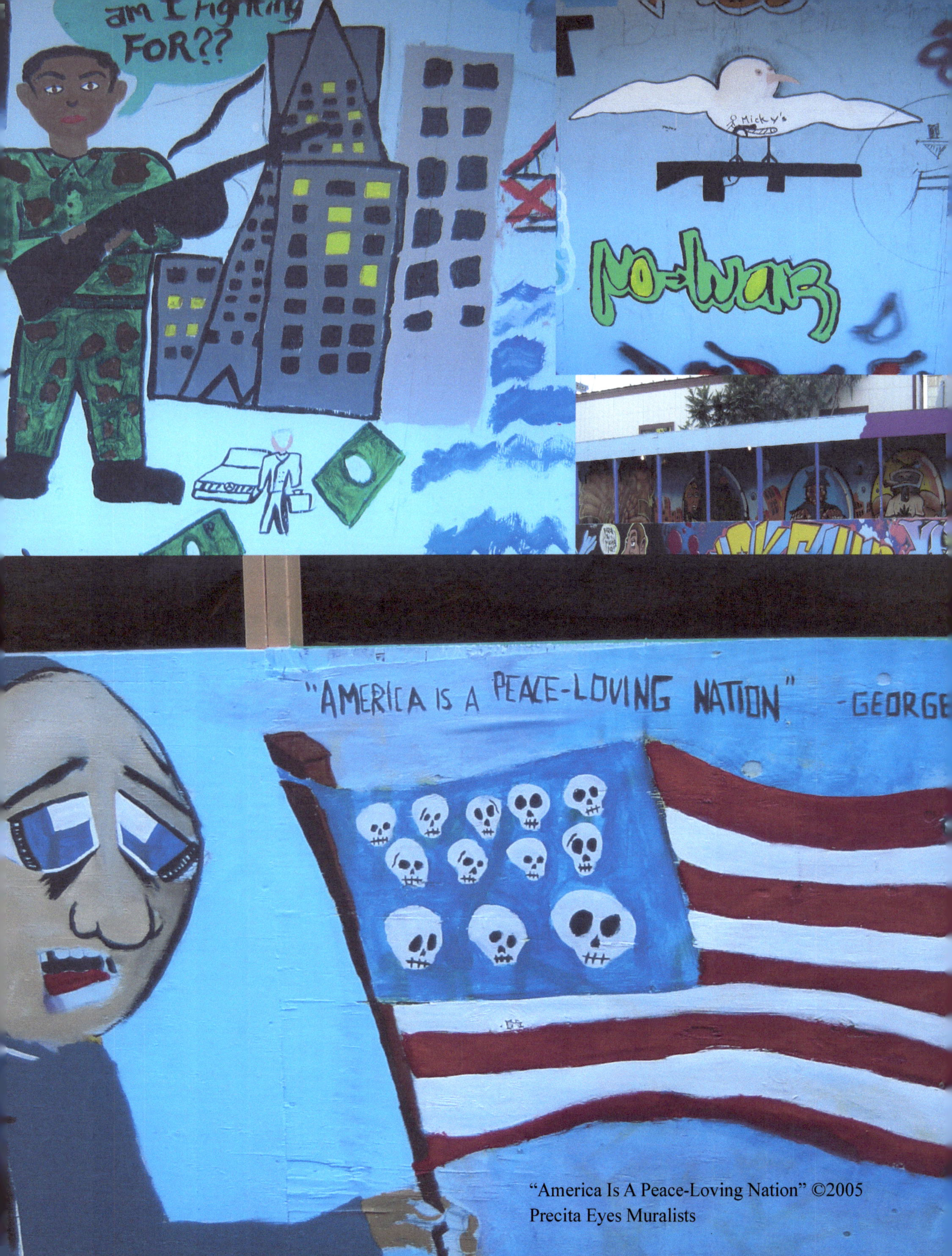

"America Is A Peace-Loving Nation" ©2005
Precita Eyes Muralists

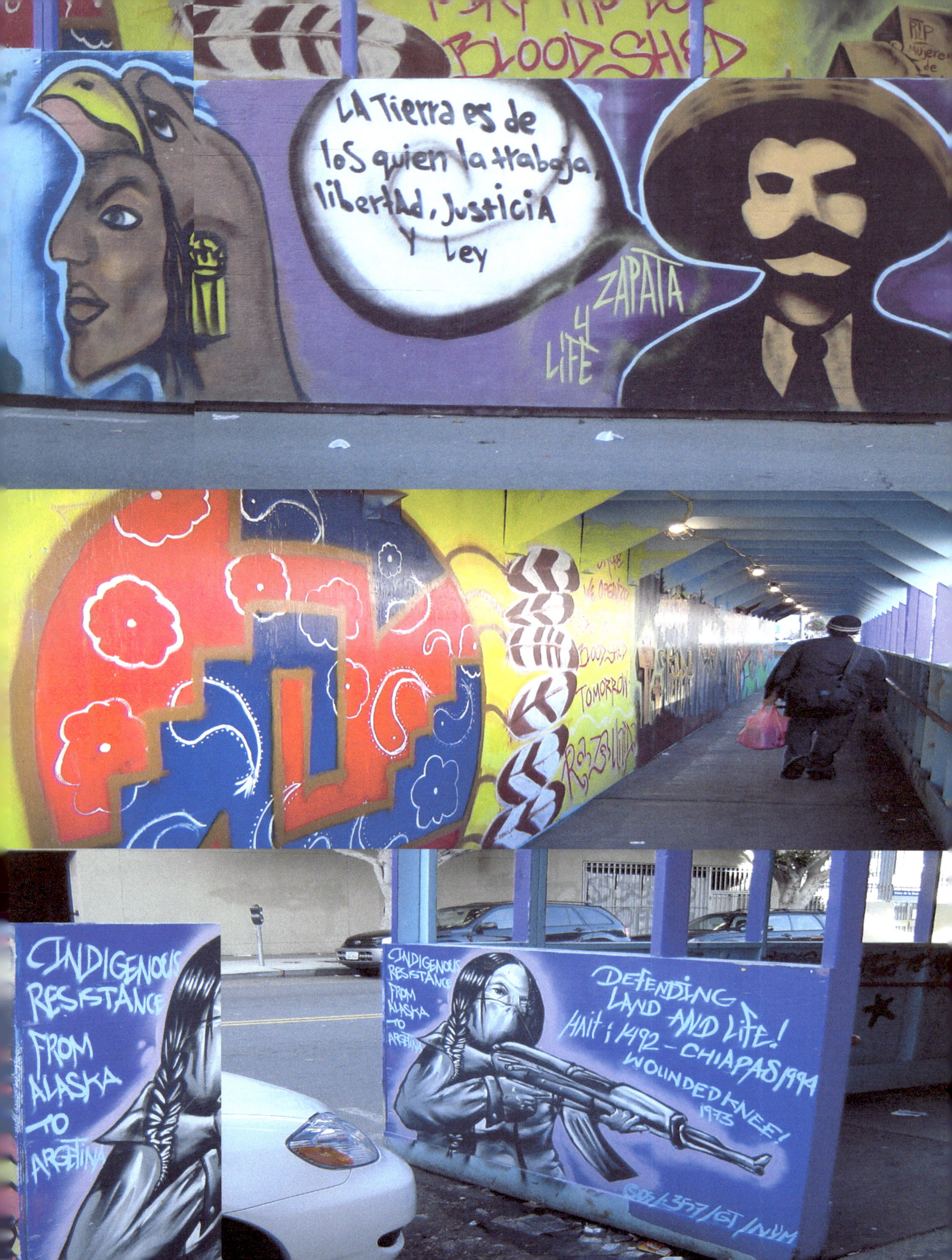
BLOODSHED
LA Tierra es de los quien la trabaja, libertAd, Justicia Y Ley
ZAPATA 4 LIFE
WE ORGANIZE
BLOODSHED
TOMORROW
INDIGENOUS RESISTANCE FROM ALASKA TO ARGETINA
INDIGENOUS RESISTANCE FROM ALASKA TO ARGETINA
DEFENDING LAND AND LIFE!
Hait i 1492 - CHIAPAS 1994
WOUNDED KNEE! 1973

Cross Cultural Exchange

I shudder when I think of past Mardi Gras parades. They are impossible to avoid when you live in a suburb of New Orleans, which is where I grew up. Not that I've always wanted to avoid them. I went to my first few with abundant eagerness, enough to suffer through a French kiss from a total stranger for the sake of a beautiful bead necklace. Two decades later, I still remember that kiss. I was sixteen years old and it was my first kiss and I hadn't expected to have an unwanted tongue shoved down my throat. Regardless, I went back to the parades the next day, and the next year, and the year after...

I find it difficult to reconcile my current self with the one that desperately competed for Mardi Gras beads, doubloons, and the various other trinkets that people riding on the floats throw down to people in the street watching the parade. Once, in my enthusiasm, I stepped on the hand of a young child as he reached down to grab a doubloon. After that, I took a break from the parades. At least until the next year. Even when I didn't want to go, the pressure from friends and everyone around me was impossible to resist.

Although I have not attended a Mardi Gras parade for over a decade, there are Mardi Gras beads in my bathroom and my bedroom. I have a wooden Dutch shoe in my kitchen that's stuffed with silver-gold-red-green-blue doubloons. They symbolize the fact that Mardi Gras is a part of my youth, part of my life in New Orleans. Thus, it was with a mix of nostalgia and curiosity that I went to see the documentary "Mardi Gras: Made in China," about the origins of the Mardi Gras beads and other trinkets. Of course they are "Made in China." Isn't everything? I had read in the Times Picayune, the local New Orleans newspaper, that the beads are made in China and India. This explained why they could be bought so cheaply and thrown out for free to the revelers. So, when The Artists' Television Access (ATA) on Valencia Street in the Mission scheduled a screening of the film, I wanted to find out more.

The documentary tells the story of the lives of the mostly female workers in the bead factories of China. Many of them are pre-teens and teenagers who work at the factory in lieu of an education. Some are not interested in an education and are happy to get out of schooling but others work because their families need and/or want the extra money. The hours are long and wages are shockingly low by US standards. This is not much of a surprise except when you compare it to the two million dollars annual salary of the factory's CEO. Workers must abide by many factory rules which are designed to make them more efficient. For example, they are not allowed to talk while working. Breaking the rules has severe consequences. One punishment is the loss of up to one week's wage. The factory workers are required to work almost seven days a week with sporadic time off.

To broaden its perspective "Mardi Gras: Made in China" traveled to the other side of the world, to New Orleans, and asked Mardi Gras spectators if they knew where and how the beads are produced. The filmmakers showed footage of the factory workers to the Mardi Gras partier. Some revelers didn't care. Some were appalled at the working conditions which made it possible for them to wear the multi-colored beads around their neck. And some thought that the Chinese wages are probably adjusted to the cost of living of that region and that what might be shockingly low salaries and unacceptable working conditions for US workers are probably appropriate for the Chinese culture and lifestyle.

They also showed footage of the Mardi Gras merrymakers to the Chinese factory workers. The footage included shots of women revealing their breasts in exchange for beads. Many factory workers were shocked that anyone would take their clothes off to obtain one of those "ugly" beads.

Looking at the factory workers, I recalled that I was the same age as many of them when I started working after school. I earned enough, however, to buy my own car that I brought with me to college. I was also the same age as many of them when I attended my first Mardi Gras parade and allowed a stranger to kiss me in exchange for the "beautiful" bead necklace he wore around his neck.

The past and the present come together for me in this one night where New Orleans comes to the Mission neighborhood at the ATA, a place where independent films often show up to provoke emotions and thoughtful responses.

Artist Television Access is located at 992 Valencia Street between Liberty and 21st Streets.

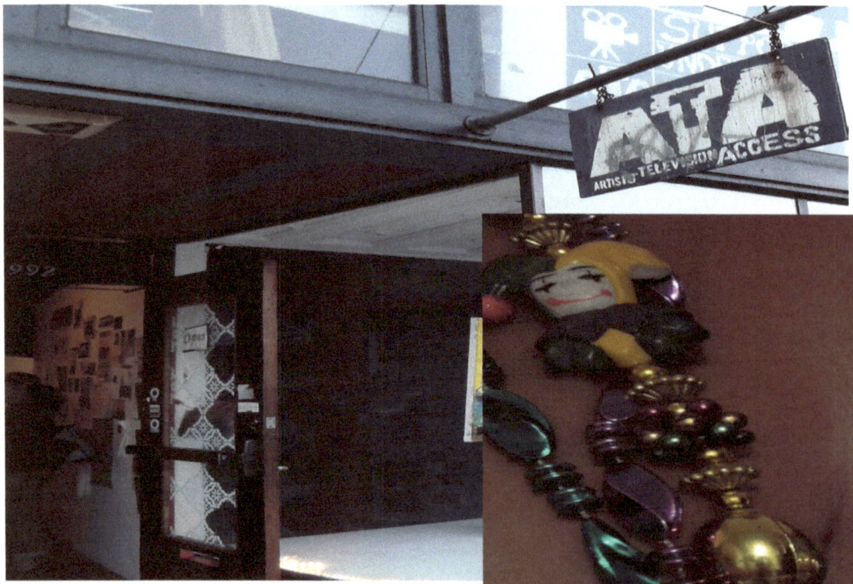

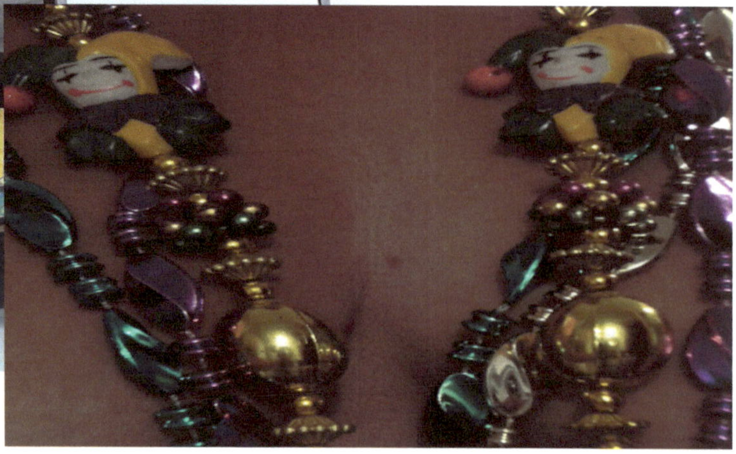

Art, Resurrected

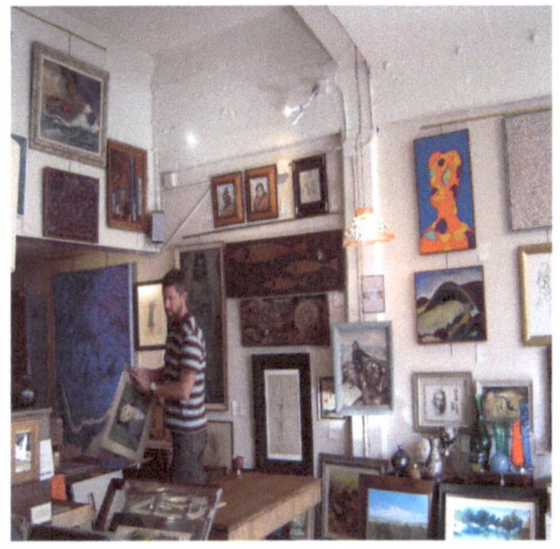

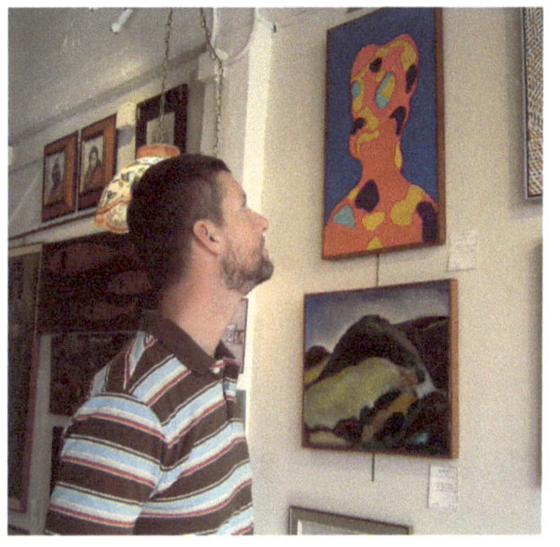

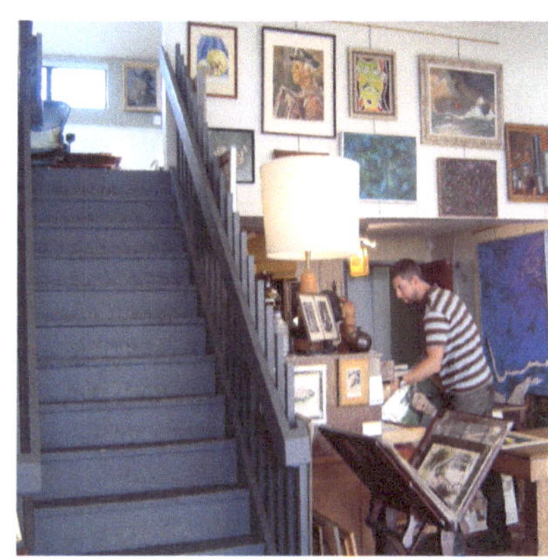

An unknown artist, Peter Witwer, is shot and killed near his home in San Francisco's Haight Ashbury neighborhood. Forty years later, his paintings are resurrected as art patrons and collectors buy most of his pieces. Witwer was part of the figurative art movement occurring in the Bay Area during his lifetime. He wasn't alive to reach the critical acclaim achieved by his contemporary figurative artists like David Parks or Diebenkorn. But, thanks to a local art gallery, Witwer's lifetime of work, bought by a friend after his death, is finally hanging on the walls of many art aficionados.

The gallery that discovered Witwer is Lost Art Salon, founded in July 2005 by Rob Delamater and Gaetan Caron. It is fashioned after 1920's Paris salons where exhibit openings were social events hosted by art patrons in their homes. In the spirit of those salons, Rob and Gaetan have created a living-room setup with coffee tables, sofas, and chairs where visitors can relax with a cup of tea during a visit. For new exhibits openings, the owners throw parties with food, drink, and festivities that often include live performances ranging from flamenco to vaudeville acts.

During the day, natural light filters in through the large wall-to-wall windows and illuminates the cornucopia of art in this space. The walls beckon with a diverse style of paintings, sketches, watercolors, and more. The tables and shelves and all available flat surfaces seduce the eye with an array of objects ranging from delicate glass pieces to ceramic pottery to sculptures created from a diverse set of materials. The pieces share the facts that most of the unknown/slightly known artists are dead, that the works were created between 1900 and

1969 and that they were lovingly selected by Rob and Gaetan for this unpretentious gallery.

Finding these unique objets d'art entails a lot of diligence. The gallery owners attend private sales, estate sales, and various exhibits to find something that entices them and fits their thematic setting. Sometimes family members of artists contact the salon. In the case of deceased artist Paul W. McCoy, his daughter contacted the Lost Art Salon. While alive, McCoy, a writer and editor, took off two years from work to paint bucolic scenes of the Spanish countryside. He was too shy to exhibit his pieces during his lifetime so his family never had a chance to bask in the glory of his talent. Recently, however, his wife and daughters enjoyed a Lost Art Salon art opening in his honor. As a result of that show, McCoy's pieces are hanging at the Park Hotel in San Francisco. Some of his pieces have also been featured in Williams Sonoma advertisements.

Not all the artists at the Lost Art Salon are "discovered" after their death. Rob and Gaetan stumbled across local artist Wiveca R. Rubinow via a single painting they purchased at a show in Napa. Placing a photo of the piece on their website resulted in a phone call from a Rubinow collector. The Salon acquired the collection and has been selling pieces to interested patrons. Rubinow is one of the few artists featured at the salon who made money from her art while still alive.

Gallery clientele range from private collectors, independent filmmakers, and interior designers to commercial clients like Williams Sonoma, Pottery Barn, and Tommy Hilfiger. Priced at under one thousand dollars, including framing, the pieces are affordable for young aspiring collectors. The art rental fees are also reasonable for independent filmmakers and attractive to commercial clients who want to rent the pieces for a particular show. Some clients come because they are looking for a particular theme or for period pieces.

This is not to say that all pieces at the salon cost less than $1000. Some of the pieces cost

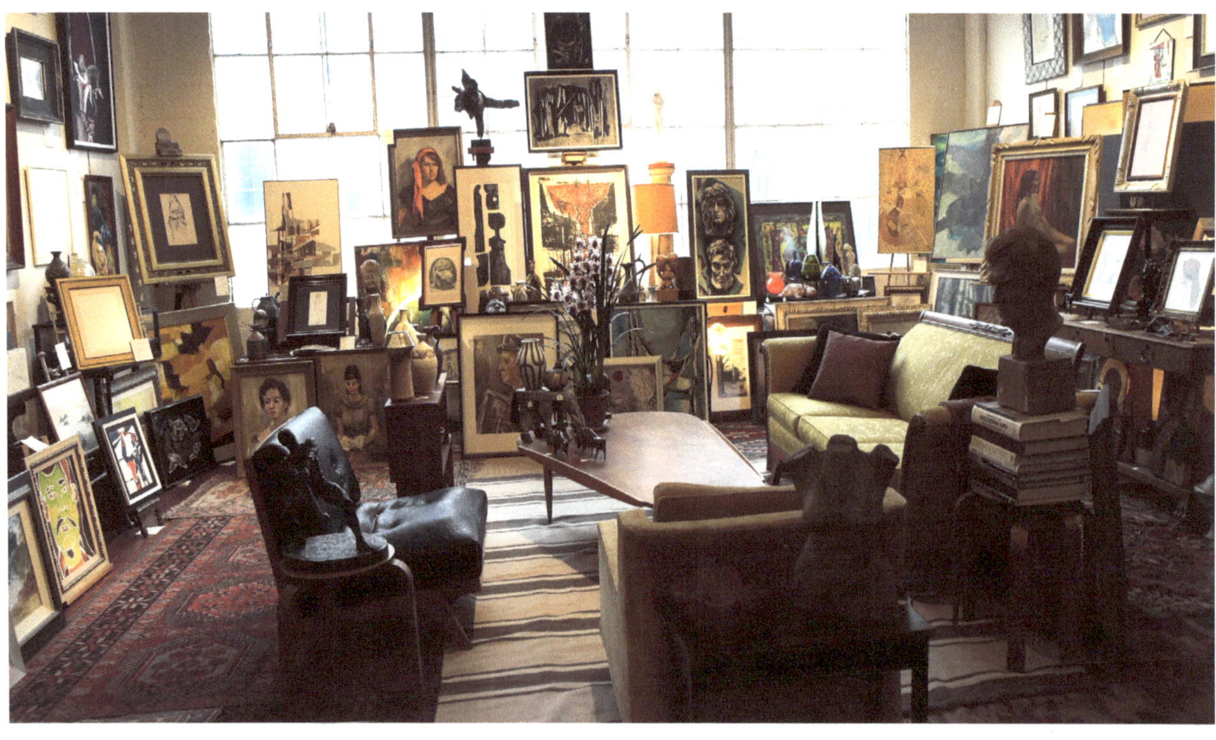

more because the artist is well known. For instance, the owners accidentally discovered woodcut pieces by Vernon E. Smith, an artist who has exhibited at the New York Museum of Modern Art and at the Smithsonian. The pieces would have gone unnoticed if it hadn't been for the fact that the renter of a storage space defaulted on payment and the owners auctioned off all the items. Luckily for Rob and Gaetan, the Smith pieces were included in this sale. It's ironic that the storage space renter could not afford to pay rent on the space because each of these pieces is now priced in the range of $3000-$4000.

There are compelling stories behind many of the works of art at this Mission space. The owners were inspired to open the gallery after collecting period pieces as a hobby; so, they have their own stories to tell about the journey that has led to full-time dream jobs for them. Ask them about the various collections and be prepared to hear stories that will raise your spirits in empathy for the artists whose talents and passion are being resurrected in this cozy and friendly art salon.

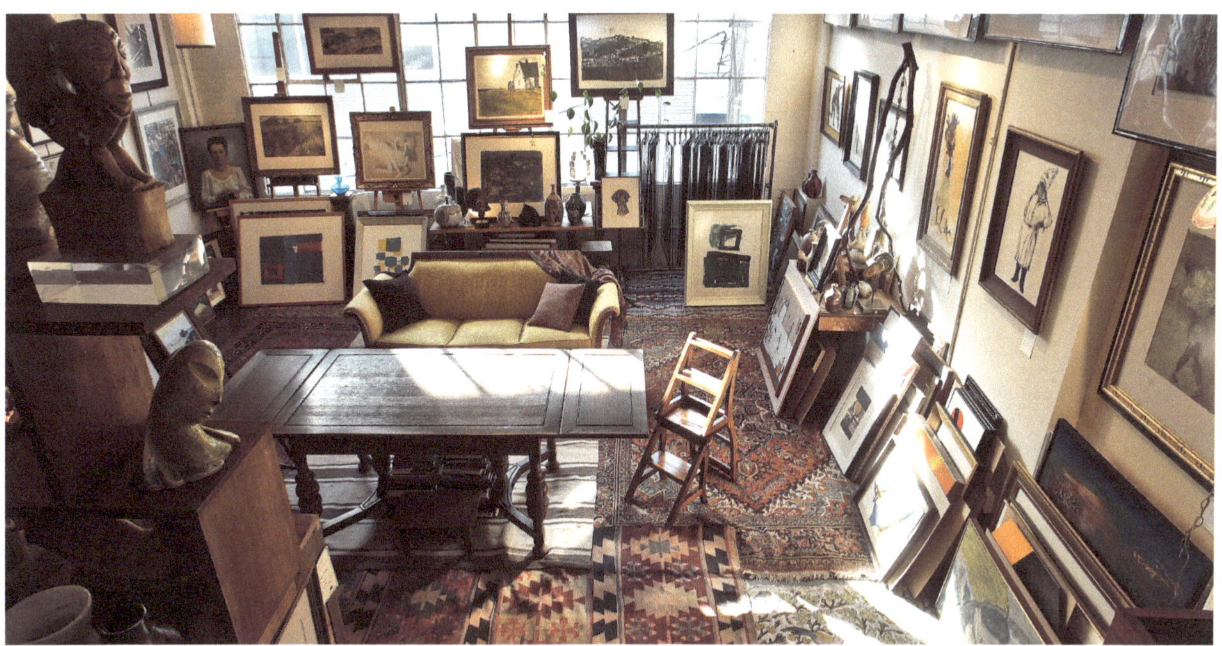

The Lost Art Salon, http://www.lostartsalon.com, is located at 245 South Van Ness #303 at the corner of 13th Street.

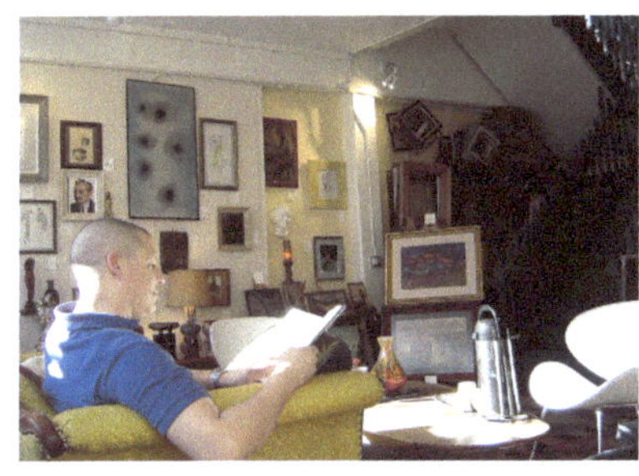

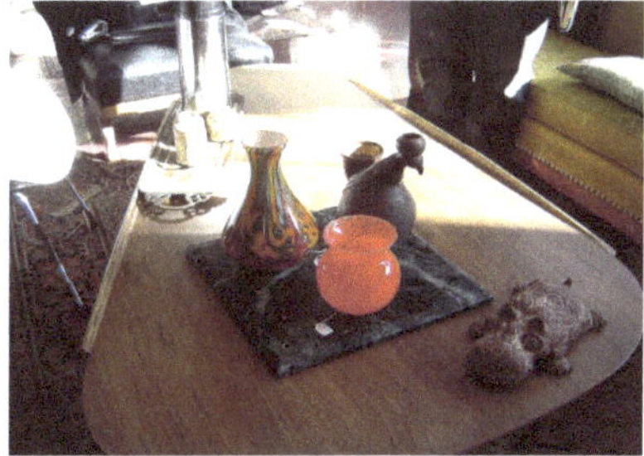

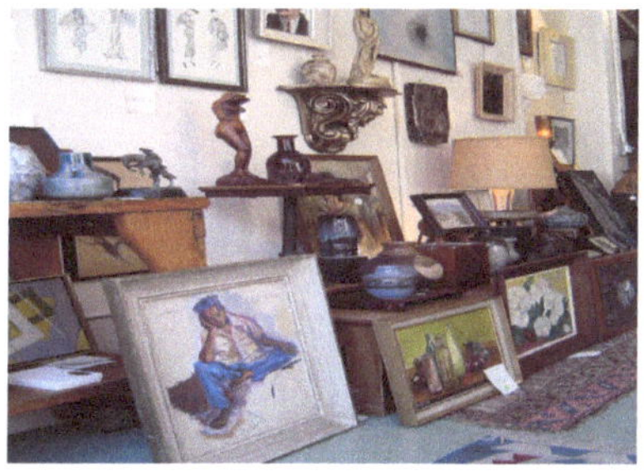

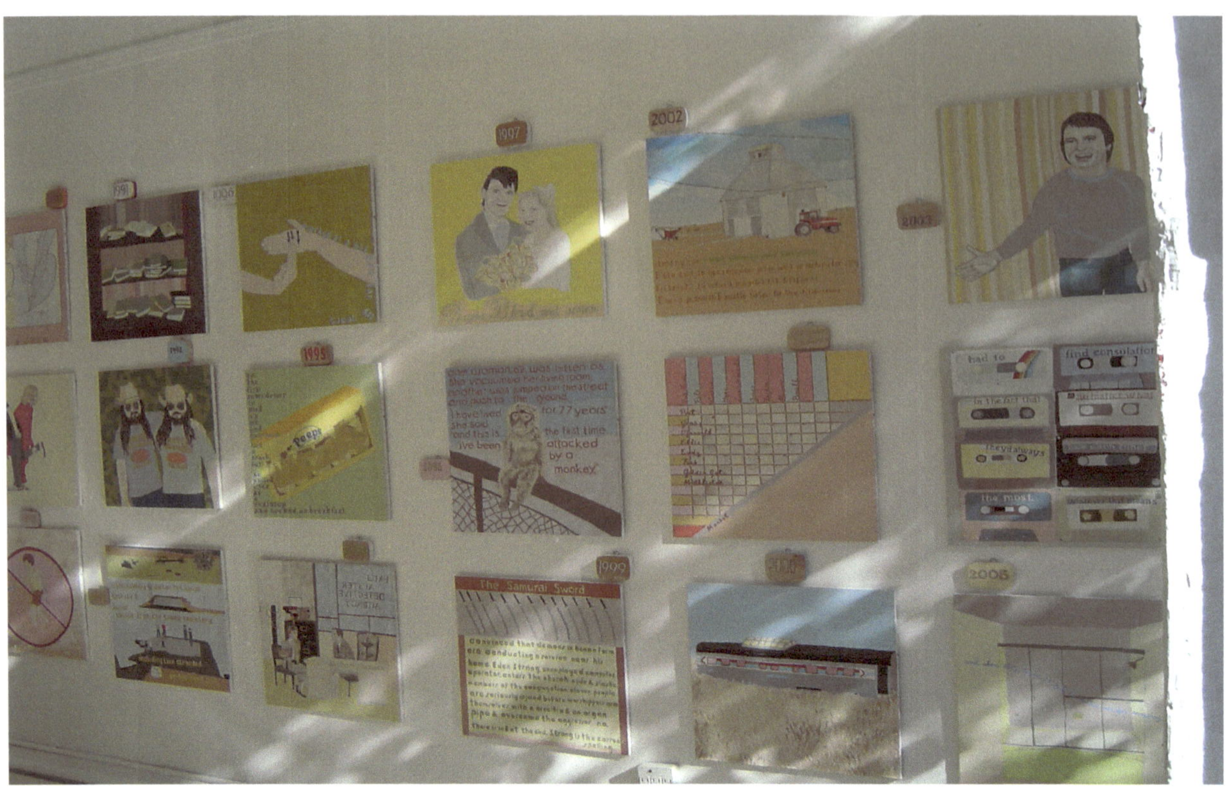

Please Come In

hello stranger who is walk'n by
and never really goes into galleries

These words, stenciled out of paper and taped to the outer glass walls of a tiny gallery, compel me. I walk in and look at the thirty-two paintings in the "A Strange 31 Years" show. I look again. There is John Ritter smiling from a painting labeled "2003: john ritter murdered? (theory of everything)." There is a woman sitting on a sofa and looking straight at me through her 3D glasses, as if I was the 3D object of her curiosity. There is a row of smiling stiff children, dressed in starched clothing, who remind me of grade school photographs where we all looked straight at the camera and presented our awkward and innocent smiles…

Intrigued, I start a conversation with the man sitting at a desk in the gallery behind a large computer screen. Brent, 27 (at the time the column was written), the co-owner of the gallery tells me that he and his business partner, Forest, 28 (at the time the column was written), founded the gallery only six months ago to showcase the works of many of their San Francisco emerging artist friends and acquaintances. Now, the gallery is booked for shows up to six months in advance and they get more requests for art shows than they can handle. But getting people to come inside the gallery has been a bit of a challenge.

"People are unaware of how much they like art," says Maria, the creator of "A Strange 31 Years" series. I had setup an appointment to meet her at the gallery after my initial conversation with Brent and Forest. She is referring to the fact that art is inherent in clothing, in everyday decorations that people place inside their homes, and even in the design of common household appliances. Her sentiments resonate with mine in the philosophy that art is a democratic, living, breathing everyday experience and not something only for the art-educated elite.

Maria lives in the Mission and is a graduate of the San Francisco Art Institute. She created the paintings in this exhibit with the vision that art should be "engaging, not confusing for the viewer or therapeutic for the artist, but friendly, open, and about something that people can read and see." This series encompasses 32 paintings, each representing one year of her life. Some of the paintings are self-referential; others depict news events and iconic references. The paintings comprise a mixture of drawing, etching, and cartoon sensibilities. Their two-dimensional approach along with a generous sprinkling of words imbue them with an urban street sensibility.

Brent and his business partner, Forest, fund the gallery with income from their jobs and hope to change the notion that art is expensive and inaccessible. Their goal is to encourage people to walk in, look around, and simply enjoy the paintings without feeling as if the price of entry is the purchase of an art-piece. Of course, they would love to sell the art too, which is why the paintings are reasonably priced. For example, Maria's pieces are $500 each.

Brent and Forest want to introduce all of San Francisco and The Bay Area to local emerging artists. To this end, they plan on bringing people into their gallery via artists' podcasts, wine-tastings and other social events. They also plan to host "Little Tree Blush," art-based events curated by Little Tree Gallery at local bars, restaurants, corporations, and other organizations.

So, don't be shy. Step into this friendly little gallery and say hi to Brent or Forest, whoever happens to be there. Enjoy the art, ask questions and if you really fall in love with a piece of art be assured that it will not cost your life savings.

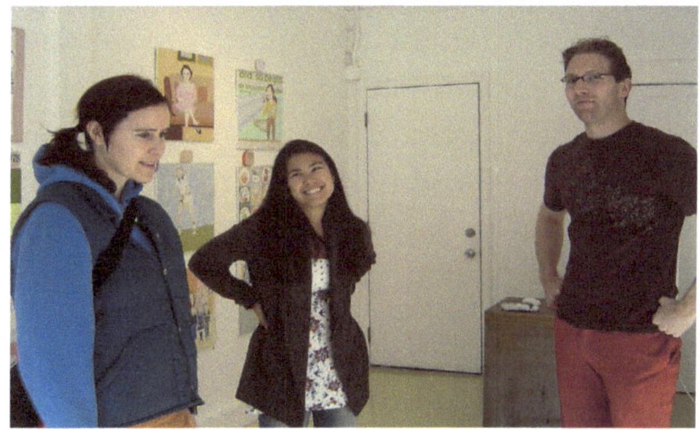

Maria, Forest, Brent

Maria Forde has a website at http://www.MariaForde.net. The Little Tree Gallery (http://www.littletreegallery.com.) is at 3412 22nd Street near Guerrero Street.

Poetic Pictures

The teenage poet is unable to stop her eyes from watering as she reads a poem about her dead friend. Her loss becomes so tangible in those tears that the source and inspiration of her writing suddenly becomes clear to me and I understand that poetry has given her a home of sorts, a place to not only grieve but also to find solace. I can't say that I understand her pain but I am touched by her sorrow.

This reading took place at a recent Poetry Slam at The Intersection for the Arts. The poets ranged from Junior High students and their teachers, to professional poets like Ruth Forman, author of "We Are the Young Musicians and Renaissance." According to Booklist, Ruth Forman's poems are "alive and kicking; they pound and pulse with a hard-won sense of self, beauty, femininity, strength and righteous indignation…" Ruth Forman personifies her poems as she captivates the audience with not just her word craft, but also with a spirited delivery that makes the words of Booklist come alive for the audience.

The visual element at a poetry reading is, of course, the physical presence of the poet and an emotional delivery that hints at the genesis of the poem. The narrative element is a combination of the poet's personality and ability to connect the message of the poem to the emotions of the audience. For example, one of the poets at the reading wrote about how Mexicans are found behind-the-scenes in every eating establishment in San Francisco, but rarely in the forefront as managers, hosts, or waiters. In the fashion of a Poetry Slam, the poet reads with emotion and flourish and with a touch of humor. He also mentions his Mexican heritage in the poem. There is a poignancy to his reading that would not have affected me with the same force if I had read those words silently in my head from a black and white piece of paper.

Of course, there were occasional readings where I dozed off for a second or longer. It wasn't necessarily that the poem was unappealing but that the poet's delivery lacked charisma. But, it's difficult to clearly ascribe the lack of appeal to the poem itself or to the poet's lack of personal magnetism. This being a Poetry Slam, I expected performance and consequently lost interest when the poet did not use the force of their voice, appearance, and personality to tap into the visual and narrative potentials of their poem.

On the contrary, it was impossible not to pay full attention to the poet who read with ardent convictions about her feelings regarding the Iraq war and racism.

I wonder if the poets are affected by the audience response. The listening crowd laughs, sighs, cheers, and claps. As a fan of poetry, it is reassuring to witness its revival and to experience the reading of poetry as a social phenomenon rather than a silent and solitary affair.

I hadn't expected to write about the Poetry Slam as part of a visual narrative series. The experience convinces me that there's a visual and narrative element to Poetry Slams. This explains its popularity over traditional poetry readings that focus on just the words of the poem and not the poet.

It wasn't until Poetry Slams invaded the urban landscape that poetry became a visual experience. Of course, MTV added a visual dimension to songs a long time ago. But, it is Poetry Slams that bridged the gap between poetry as an exclusive domain of the elite and that of the urban masses by putting poets on the stage as not just readers but as presenters of the poem.

A poet's work is to name the unnameable, to point at frauds, to take sides, start arguments, shape the world, and stop it going to sleep.

Salman Rushdie

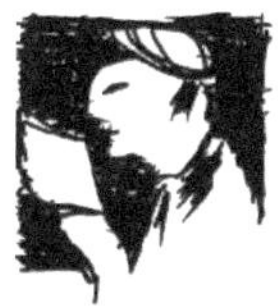

The Intersection for the Arts at 446 Valencia Street near 16th Street.

Visual Feast

Things happen, things that might shift your focus for a few seconds, a few minutes, or more. I have one of those moments as I pass by Radio Habana Social Club and am compelled to look. The place is not open for business. It's the outside front wall that rivets my attention.

There are so many things for my eyes to feast on that I don't know where to start. Is that a tiny skeleton hanging in the window? Oh, there's a statue of Snow White, next to a bearded man in denim overalls, and there's a dwarf, and Virgin Mary...How is it possible that nobody has stolen these? That's when I notice the nail through Snow White's skirt and through each foot of the man in overalls, and between Mary's feet...Below the sculptures, there is a still life painting of a Mayan statue, also nailed to the outside walls. To the right of the painting, an assortment of wooden objects (a cat, a fish, a dinosaur, a cigar) are nailed to a small shelf....then a STOP sign. An actual stop sign, customized with a sketch of the Statue of Liberty, is on the shelf.

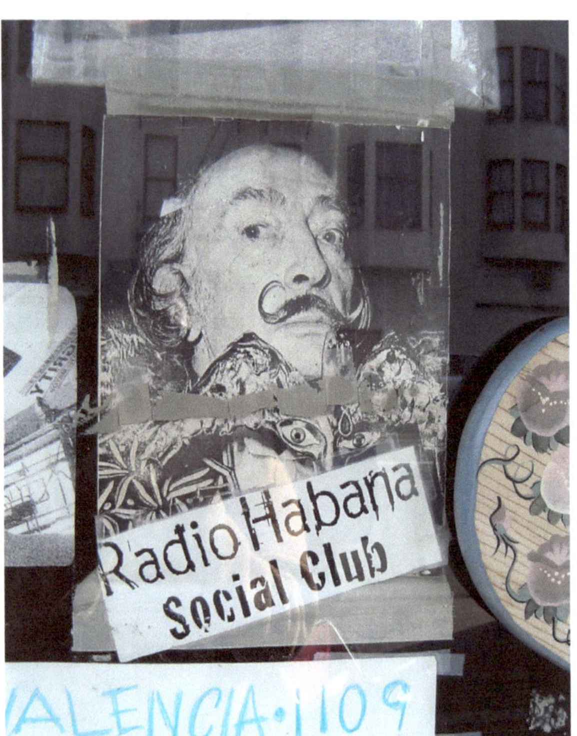

My eyes move to the single crutch with an ice-skating shoe attached to the bottom. I wonder if there is a story here. Was the skate responsible for the crutch? My eyes travel left towards the window and pass over a twelve inch wooden fork and knife crossed over each other with a broken pink skull in the V between them. On the shelf below, a plastic Donald Duck plays with a car while Mickey Mouse looks on.

As I keep gazing, I can no longer dismiss the chaotic collection of unusual objects because they are starting to appeal to my appreciation of surrealist and dada art. Would any of these objects survive by itself if put up on a wall in a gallery? I've seen less compelling collages celebrated in prestigious institutes like the SFMoMA, many of which haven't evoked my senses in the same manner as this collection. Perhaps this entire place is an objet d'art, I muse to myself.

I return to Radio Habana, another day, to look at the inside walls. The indoor paintings and artwork further support my earlier theory that surrealism and its relative dada had been the sources of inspiration behind this unusual Mission icon.

On one of the inside walls, a giant pink wig looms large on a mannequin head of a woman wearing sunglasses, hot pink lips, and pearl necklaces. Her head is arranged to pop out of the wall at a thirty degree angle. Above the bar, a sculpture of a woman in black leather and Mohawk competes for attention with a plastic chicken hanging from the ceiling. A spider web with the face of a woman in the center hangs on the front wall of the restaurant... everywhere I look or point my camera, there is a visual treat.

I can barely turn my eyes away from the art to look at the menu. I let my friends order for me. The food is delicious. A vegetarian friend is able to order an entire platter and everything is priced under $10. Someone orders plates of samosas and salad. I have a tamale but I am too mesmerized by the walls to pay close attention.

The menu boasts that this is the "Best Place for Sangria, Revolutionary Talk & Spontaneous Singing" but I'll probably come back here to stimulate my appetite for dada and surrealist extravagance.

Radio Habana Social Club is located at 1109 Valencia Street, near 22nd Street.

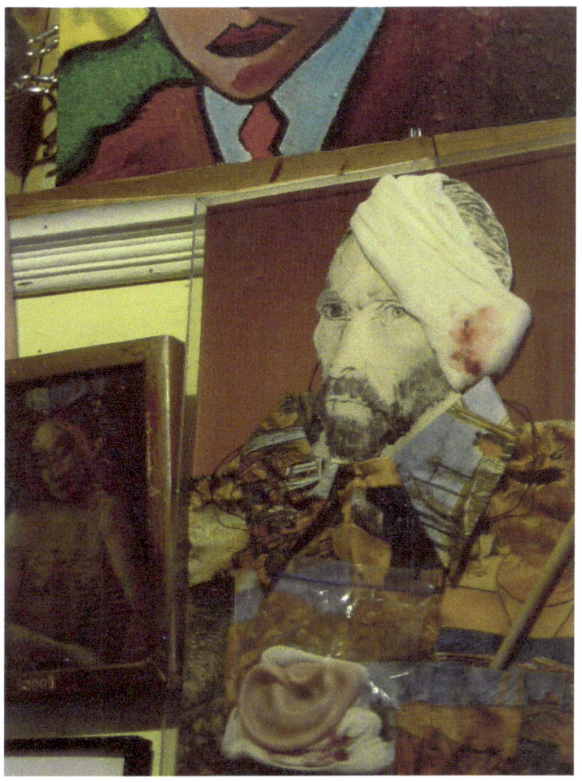

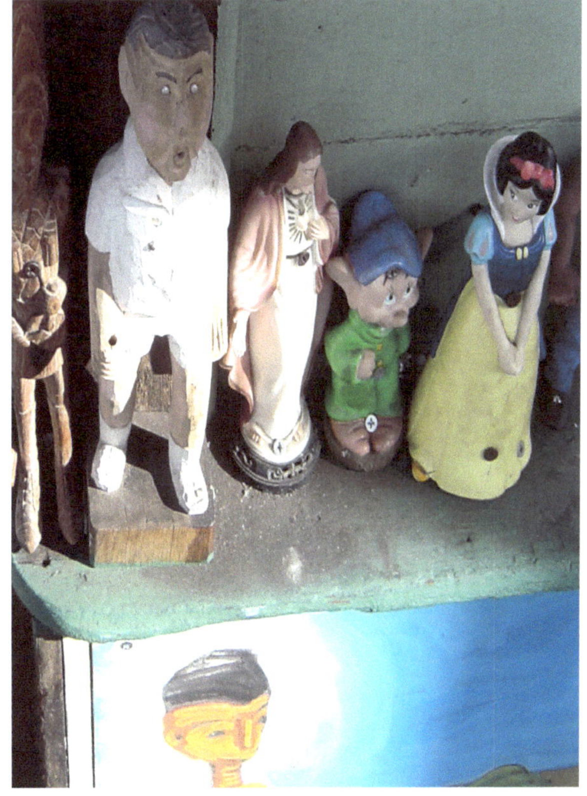

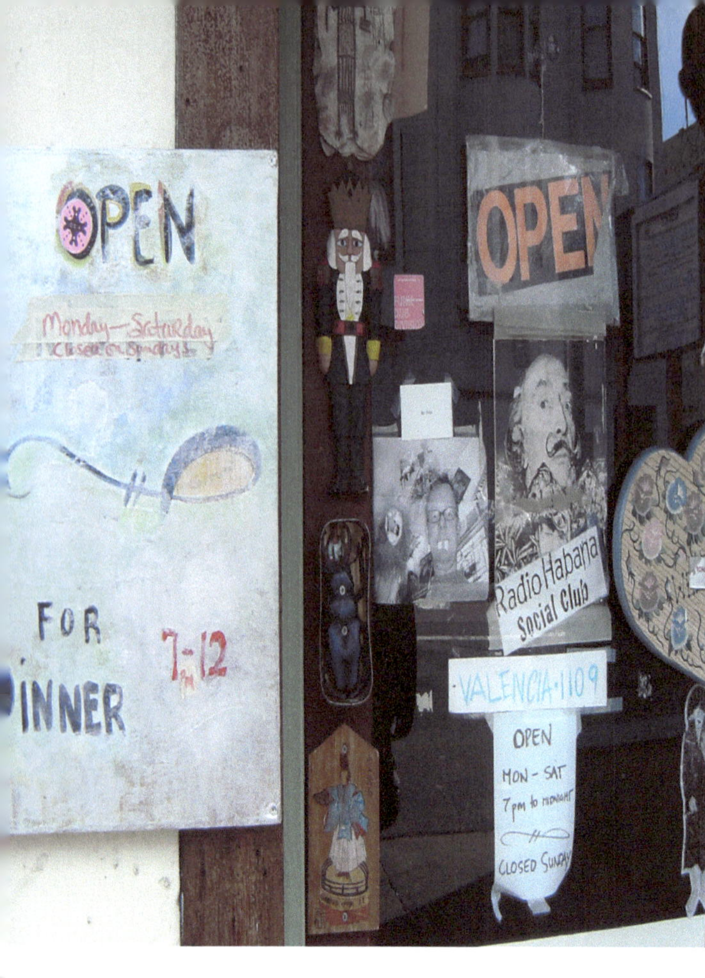
OPEN
Monday—Saturday
closed on Sundays
FOR
INNER
7pm 12
OPEN
Radio Habana
Social Club
VALENCIA 1109
OPEN
MON - SAT
7pm to midnight
CLOSED SUNDAY

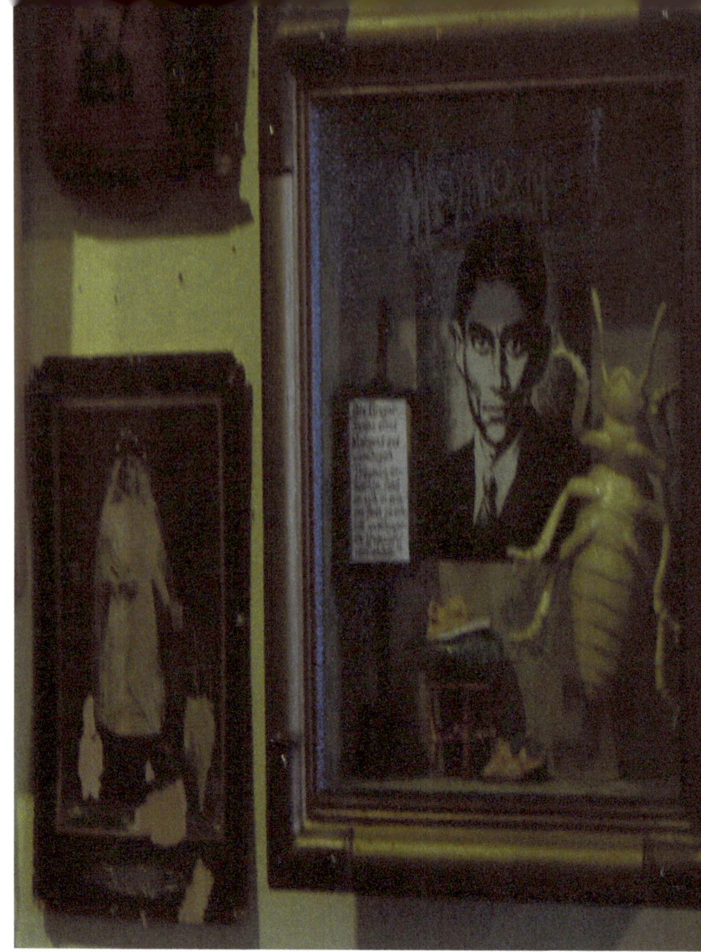

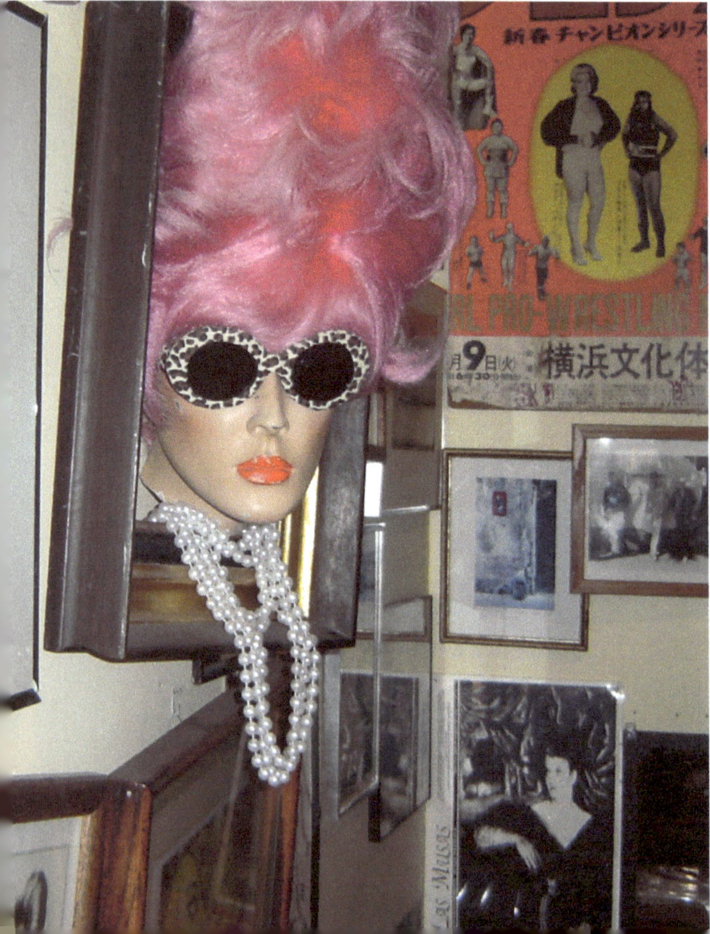
新春チャンピオンシリーズ
9日(火)
横浜文化体

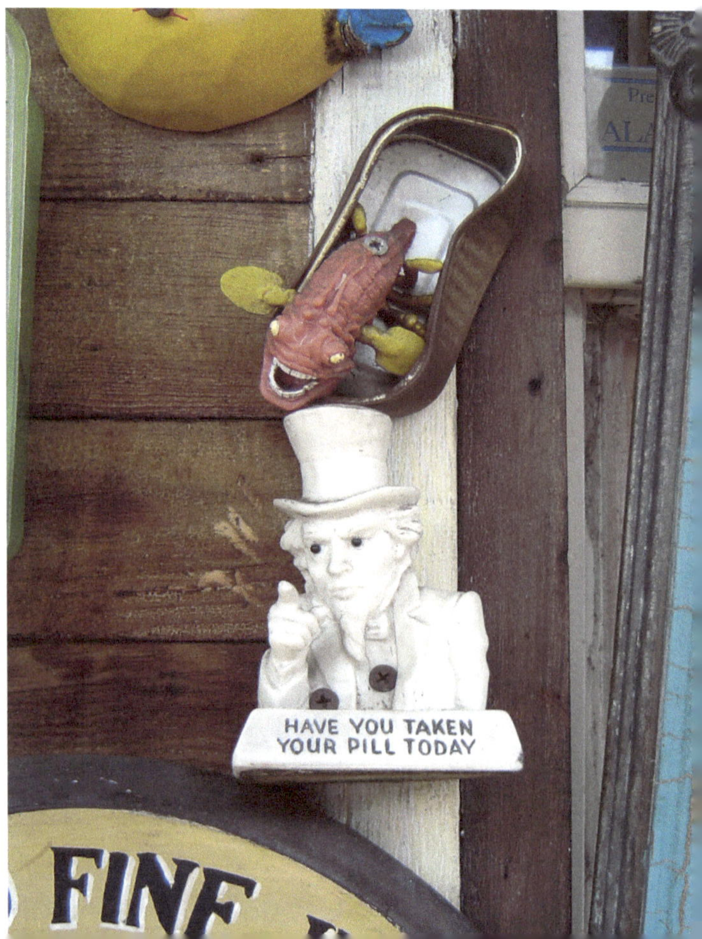
HAVE YOU TAKEN
YOUR PILL TODAY
FINE

The Artist Next Door

When you see the paintings, photographs and other visual art ubiquitous in San Francisco restaurants and coffeehouses, do you wonder where they came from? Are you aware that the artist might be your next-door neighbor or the young gal sitting next to you on the bus or the middle-aged man waiting behind you in the grocery line? There are so many artists in San Francisco that most of you probably know at least one and might even have a friend whose art you see regularly at your favorite café.

I'm one of those artists whose works you might see around town. Among the places where I show my work is at the Art Explosion's monthly "Sneak Peek", an event which is open to the public.

"You want THAT?!" The words rolled out of my mouth. I was shocked that someone wanted to pay money for one of my photographs (the one on the cover). "It's wonderful. I love the composition and the local color," the guy said, as if defending my piece, a photograph of words in red paint scrawled across a crumbling gray wall. He handed me thirty-five dollars. Still dumbfounded, I couldn't figure out the change. "It's four dollars," he said.

That was the first photograph I sold. I'm a painter and a photographer but hadn't made any efforts to show my pieces until the Sneak Peek started happening at the Art Explosion studios where I rent an art studio. Participating in these shows has encouraged me to create more art and consider showing them at local galleries and coffee houses.

Jeremy Sutton, a Sneak Peek participant, makes a living as an artist. His large-scale digital-based multi-media portraits are a consistent presence at the monthly show. He sells many of his pieces by commission, has written books on art, and teaches art classes.

Another regular participant, Russ McCabe, shows photographs ranging in size from 5x5 black and white prints to large landscapes that resemble paintings. At a recent Sneak Peek, an art gallery owner showed interest in showcasing Russ's work. "The monthly event creates a laid back atmosphere that brings in the busy Mission foot traffic of people who may not normally make it to a gallery opening," says McCabe.

Sneak Peek is a great place for the artists and the general public to connect. I love answering questions posed by other artists and by the attendees. Most of the host artists are friendly and accessible. Although some artists are shy about socializing, they are usually happy to talk about their work. Some visitors stop by because they were passing by the studios and saw the "open studios" sign; others come because of the Craigslist posting; several of my friends also show up to see my latest pieces.

If you go, it's possible that you may not connect to anything you see. Or, you may connect so much that you open up your wallet and take something home. Most of the artwork is affordably priced ranging anywhere from $10 to $1000. On more than one occasion, gallery owners have made a purchase at the show.

Who knows? You might meet the next Pablo Picasso or Frida Kahlo or David Choe (Bay Area graffiti artist) at one of these shows or you might even be inspired to become one of the emerging artists with a studio space at the Art Explosion and an art show every month.

Artists don't make objects. Artists make mythologies.
Anish Kapoor

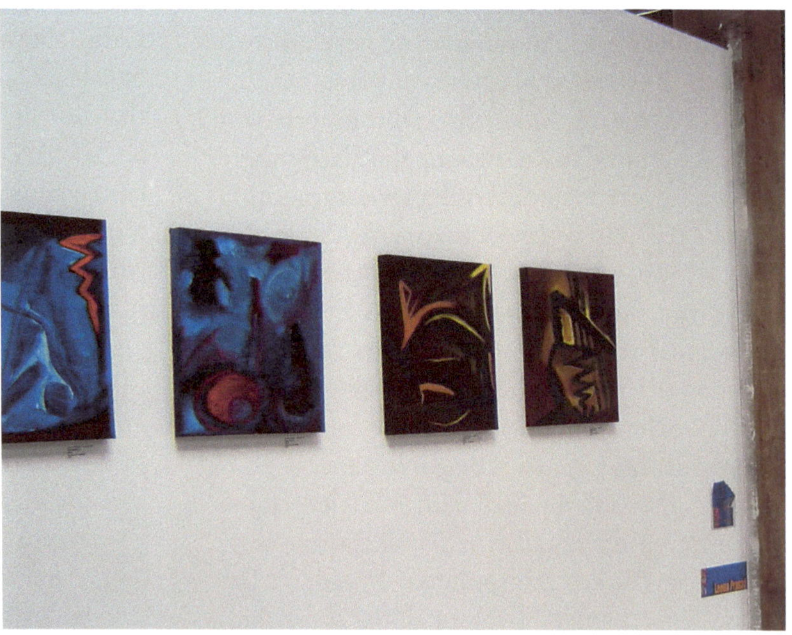

Paintings by Leena Prasad

Sneak Peak occurs at the Art Explosion studios, located at 744 Alabama Street and 2425 17th Street. Please go to http://www.theartexplosion.com/ for details.

The Roxie: a tribute

A few months ago, an artist friend told me he was moving to Oakland. He could no longer afford San Francisco rent, not even in the edgy urban artistic enclave of the Mission, on his income as a painter and a bookstore clerk. I felt sad that my friend was leaving. I also felt something else nagging at me.

It was the realization that the character of San Francisco has been changing in the last few years. It hasn't all been bad. The Mission is a lot safer than it used to be. New bookstores, restaurants, and coffee houses have added an irresistible charm to Valencia Street. I can't help but worry, however, that this change may take on a life of its own and transform the Mission into a generic commuter neighborhood with which I can no longer identify.

The way I feel about my friend leaving town is similar to how I feel when I read that the Roxie theatre on 16th Street is in danger of disappearing. Does this foreshadow a change in the intrinsic personality of San Francisco? The last time that the Roxie was in trouble, San Francisco pitched in with a fund-raiser supported by actor Nicolas Cage. How long can a business survive on the kindness of celebrities and sporadic fund-raisers? After all, it's a community's everyday life that sustains a movie theatre.

Has the San Francisco community changed so much that an independent, diverse, and cutting edge theatre like the Roxie is no lon-

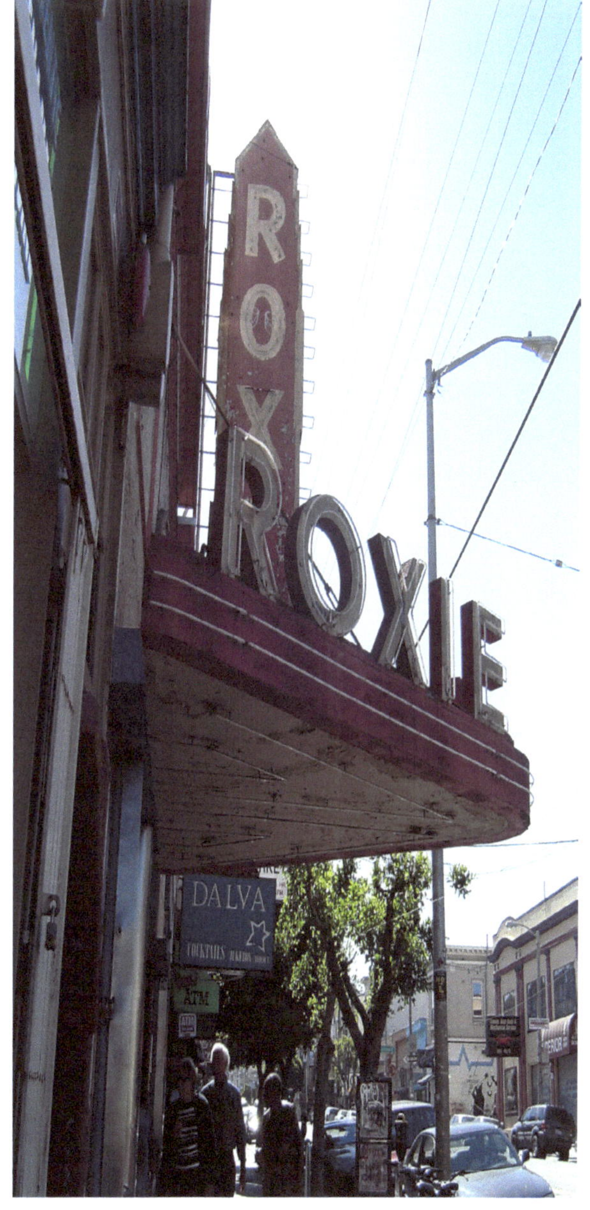

ger in demand? Besides being a Mission landmark, the Roxie is also an icon for the politics of the Mission which exemplifies San Francisco's leadership in grappling with issues that are often marginalized by mainstream media and society.

San Francisco's empathy for marginalized lives/issues is one of the reasons I chose to call this city my home. If I had unlimited time and money, I'd probably see nearly all the movies that show at the Roxie. Just look at the 2011 lineup!

So many stories, so little time!! The disappearance of the Roxie and that of my artist friend will probably leave me with cravings that would have to be satisfied with alternate options. I'll have to leave my neighborhood or troll around on the internet to satiate my hunger for visual stories that inform and challenge the mind and stretch the imagination. Thankfully, live theatres in the Mission are alive and kicking and art shows pop up all over neighborhood on a regular basis.

I'm trying to look at the Mission's artistic cornucopia as half-full but I can't help but worry if it's actually half-empty...

2011 Lineup

On The Bowery
"Lionel Rogosin's Oscar-nominated On the Bowery is a masterpiece blend of documentary and fiction. It chronicles three days on New York's skid row, the Bowery."

TWO IN THE WAVE / 'Bringing Up Léaud'
"A doc about The French New Wave that crashed onto international shores when François Truffaut's debut feature, The 400 Blows, premiered in 1959, followed by Jean-Luc Godard's Breathless, based on a Truffaut's story."

This is Noise Pop
"More than a decade in the making and featuring never-before-seen footage, This is Noise Pop explores the genesis of Indie Rock through the trials and tribulations of bands captured during and after their Noise Pop Festival performances."

Thanks to many rounds of fund-raising and generous support from Bay Area film-lover, the Roxie is still around. If you want to show your support, check out the schedule at http://www.roxie.com/ and be entertained while having your neurons exercised.

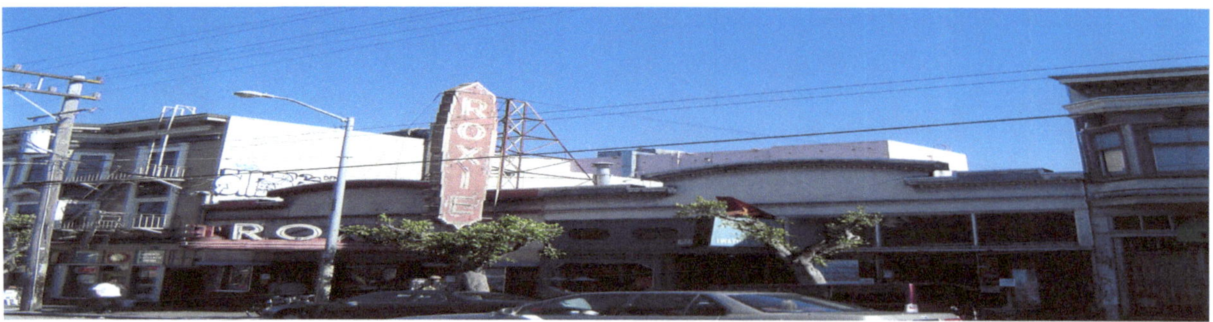

Movie Starts at Dusk

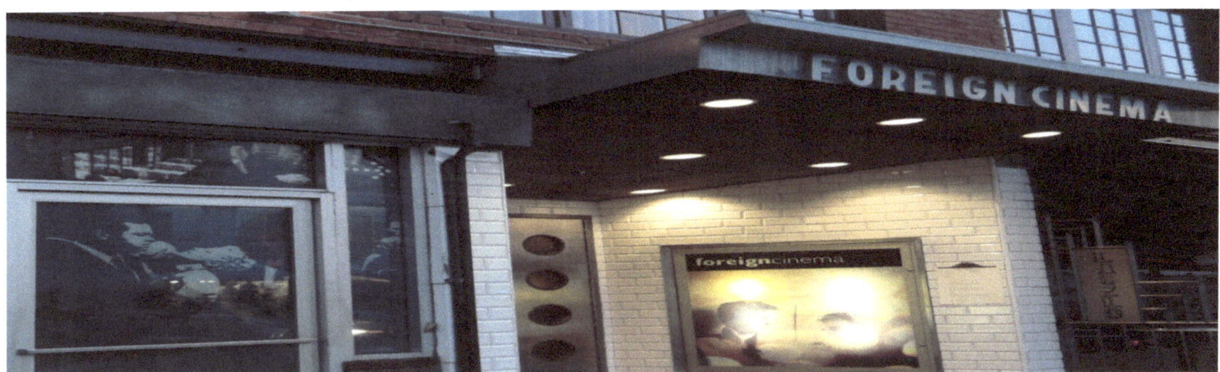

While savoring a pork chop, I turn my head to the right to see what's happening on the giant film screen: a little girl is scolding a huge ugly frog that lives inside a tree trunk. I want to keep watching but it would be rude. I'm at a birthday dinner with five other people. Then I notice that all eyes at my table have turned to watch the movie being projected onto the whitewashed brick wall. I turn the knob on the little speakers that are on a shelf above my head and raise the volume so that we can all hear the dialogue.

We are at Foreign Cinema, the Mission restaurant where dinner can easily cost $50+ per person. That's a lot of money to pay for a movie, even if it's Pan's Labyrinth. People don't come here for the film; they come here for the great food. The movie is simply part of the ambience.

This experience reminds me of another time that I had watched a film outdoors. That time, however, everyone was there for the movie Young Frankenstein. The food and alcohol that they had brought along were supplements to the film watching experience. When we were in the middle of laughing at a scene, the entire film screen deflated. The event organizers patiently put it back together and continued showing the film to the delight and amusement of the hundreds of people at Dolores Park that night. The peals of unfettered laughter increased throughout the night along with the consumption of alcohol.

As I write about these two experiences, I realize the ironic truth that the one common theme between these two places is that it's not about the film. People are likely to show up regardless of the movie that's being shown. The art of film is subsumed to the pleasure of the movie-watching experience, as an ambience factor at Foreign Cinema and as a social tool at Dolores Park.

To be fair, however, both venues do pay attention to the art of film. At Foreign Cinema, the movies selected are often independent "art" films. At Dolores Park, once a year, the movies shown are those from the independent filmmaking venture of the San Francisco 48-hour film project.

Regardless of the intentions and/or the results, Foreign Cinema and Dolores Park are both unique embodiments of The Mission spirit of meshing together art and life.

Foreign Cinema is located at 2534 Mission Street between 21st and 22nd Streets. Dolores Park is enclosed within 18th, Dolores, 20th, and Church Streets.

Walk-By Art

As I walk up 20th Street towards Dolores Park, I see him from a distance and think that he's painting the side of a wall. Something about the disarray of the paint cans and his intense posture hints at a different story. I pause as I approach and stare at the colorful mural taking shape in front of me.

He smiles when he sees me and agrees to let me take photos of his mural in progress. Encouraged by his friendliness, I ask if it would be okay to write about the mural and about him. He requests that his face be hidden in the photos and that I use his pseudonym, Octa, for the article. Why? I want to know... something

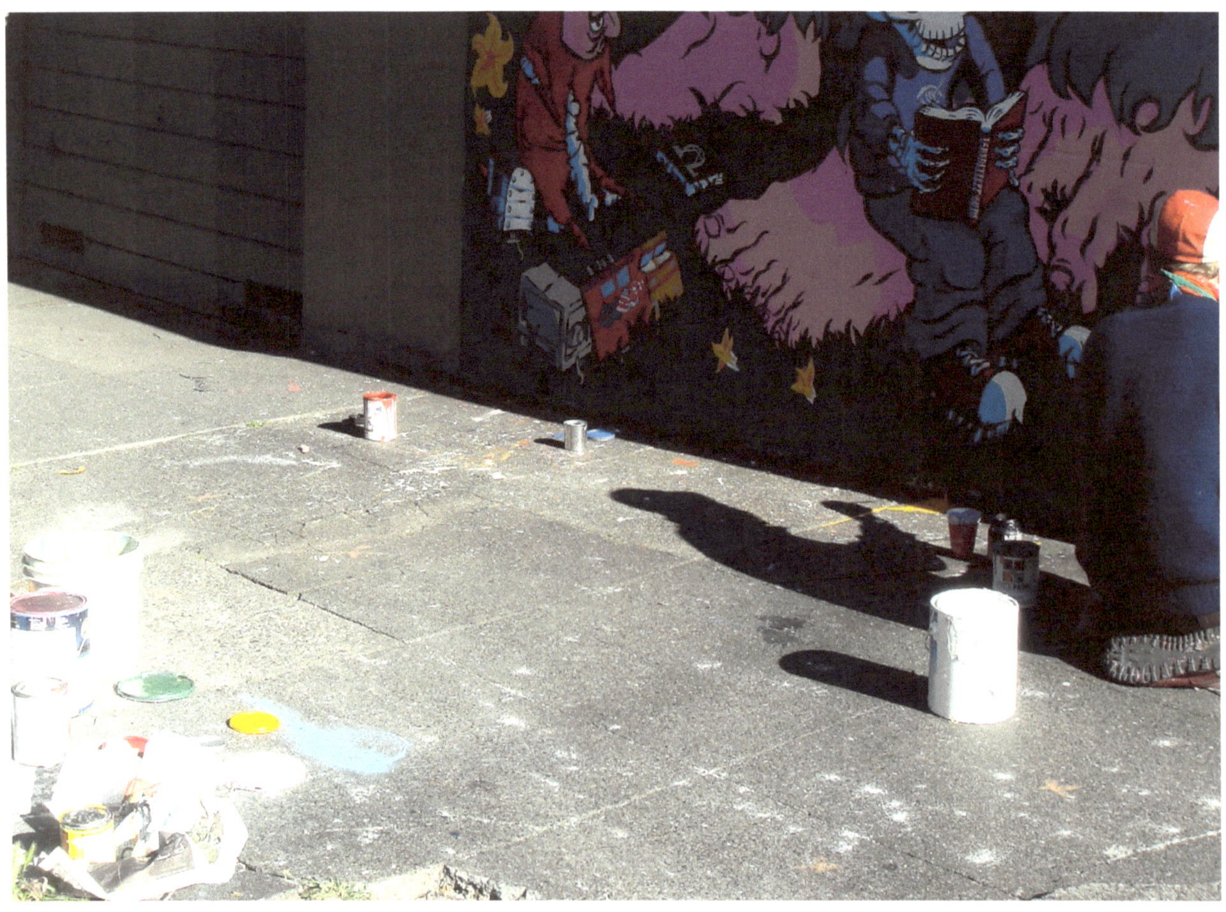

about old habits from his earlier days of being a graffiti artist, he tells me. He is an art student in Copenhagen and is staying in the Mission for four months to expand his artistic horizons.

Octa had started the painting a day earlier. Although he has only spent about twelve to thirteen hours on it so far, the mural looks almost finished. Before starting, he obtained permission from Juanita, the woman who owns the house and whose wall he is using as his canvas. He showed her some of his sketches and she picked out one that she liked. "Something that would be appropriate for my little grandchildren" was her only concern. After that, she made a decision to trust him with the details.

Juanita comes out of the house while I am talking to Octa. She says that she likes the mural and will seek out other muralists after this one fades away. As a San Francisco native who grew up with a deep sense of appreciation for outdoor murals, she was very excited when Octa knocked on her door and offered to paint a part of her wall. For free. He supplies his own paint and art material.

The mural is steeped in green and pink and has a contemporary surrealistic feel. A skeleton child with a worm in one eye socket is seated comfortably on the legs of a giant furry creature with an owlish face. The creature is lying down but his face stares out at us with a mixture of curiosity and fear. The skeleton child is reading a book.

There are other books and artifacts scattered throughout the scene, most of which have subtle references that can be interpreted differently by the viewer. I don't want to create any pre-conceived notions in your head by sharing my thoughts on these artifacts. So, take a closer look yourself by turning to the next page.

Art is the most intense mode of individualism that the world has known.

Oscar Wilde

Other works by Octa: *http://www.flickr.com/photos/uhcc.*

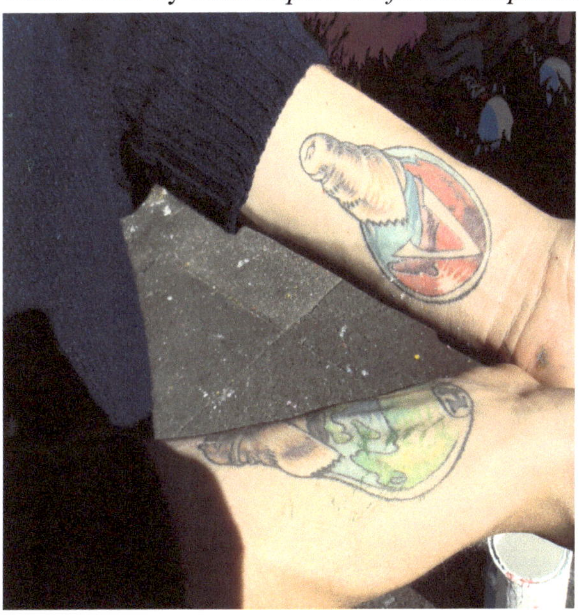

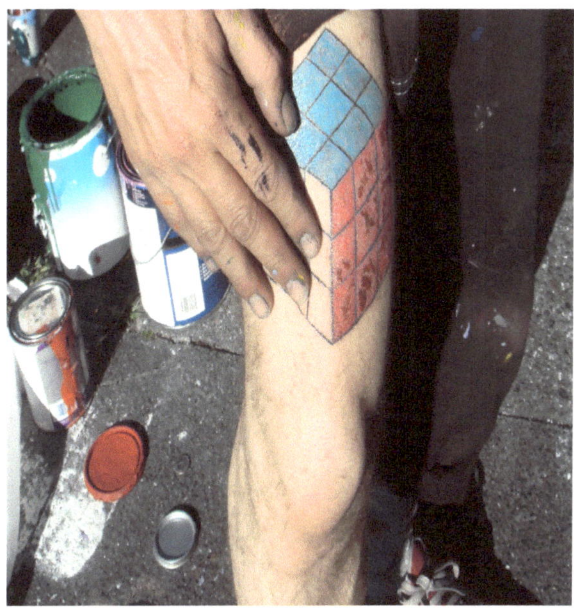

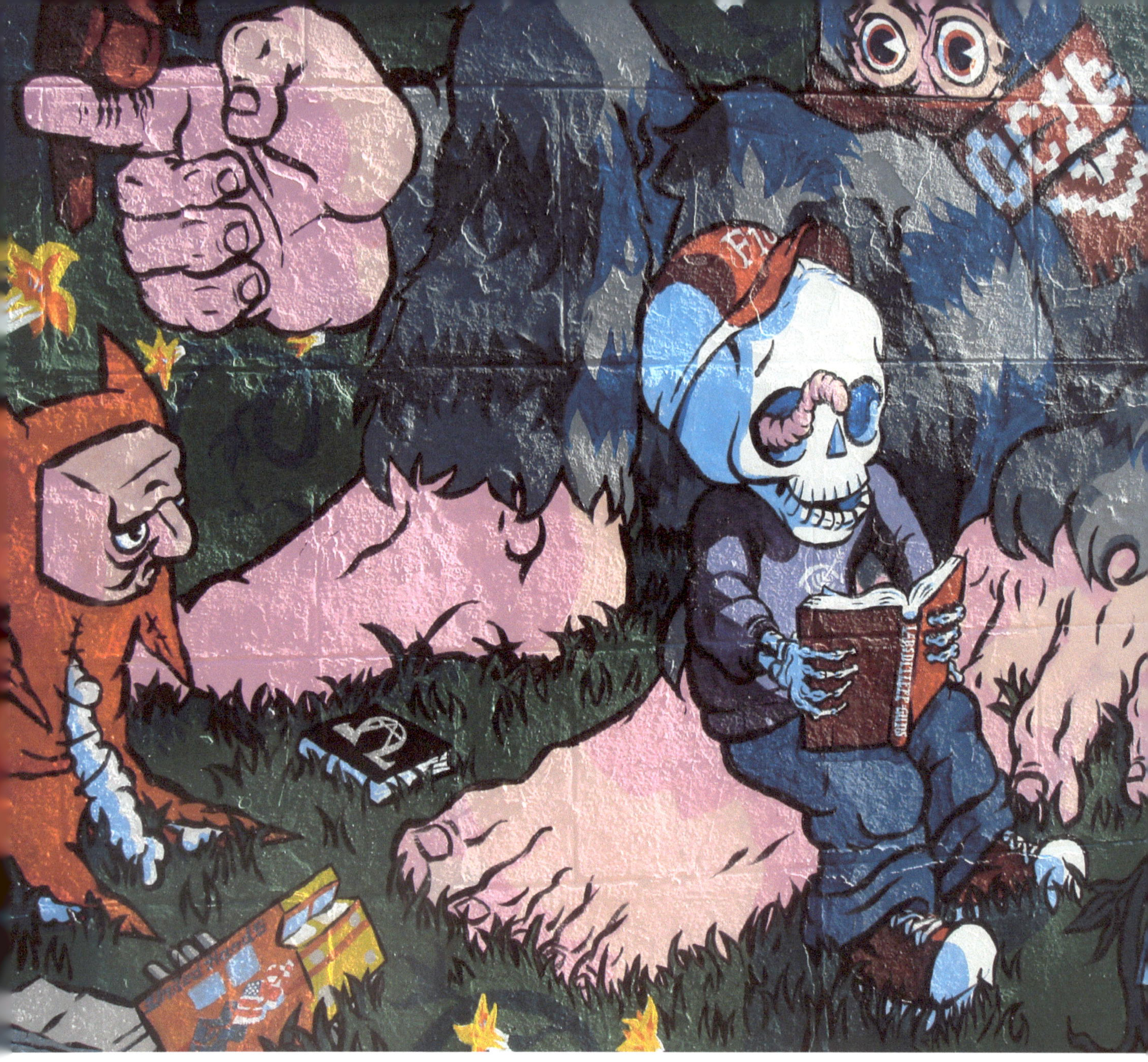

This mural was on a wall at 3647 20th Street between Valencia and Guerrero Streets. It was painted over a few months before this book went to press. For more photos go to http://community.webshots.com/user/JustShootMeNow and view the "Walk-By Art" album.

Taking It All In

Many years ago, I had an argument with my friend Sunil that art appreciation is not something that can be learned. He insisted that it could. At the time, I was not ready to listen to what he was saying.

I hadn't thought about that conversation until recently as I walked around the art studio where I rent a small space. I saw a gigantic piece of a car body hanging on the wall as part of a "found objects" exhibit. I also saw framed black and white stills from a graphic novel, giant inkblots on pieces of paper taller than my 5'2" frame, abstract art on bookmarks, photographs blurred to resemble paintings, digital photographs enhanced with digital paint and labeled as "paintings," endless sculptures of the female body in various sizes, oil paintings encased in mesh wire to symbolize the closing off of the US border…

As I walked around, I felt a new yet familiar sensation. Unlike my previous judgemental self who would have been critical and unappreciative of all the things I saw, I felt a thrill, an excitement similar to being in a foreign country and being exposed to unfamiliar visual treats. I'm maturing as an artist, I thought. I can look at art that's completely different from mine and not judge it from my point of view. I can look and appreciate these works on their own terms. I can perhaps even incorporate some of the ideas into my own work!

I suppose it's possible to learn art appreciation. But what does it take? My learning came from immersing myself in the art world for two years as an art student. How does a person who can't devote themselves to that kind of intense study learn to appreciate art or to expand their existing appreciation?

To answer this question, I thought about how people in my world look at art. I have a friend who has very little appreciation for art. She likes nature, however, and I've found her admiring the most cliched pieces of landscape as if they were masterpieces. Another friend can't "see" anything as art unless it's a perfect rendition of the real world. He appreciates my wildlife photographs but doesn't understand why I'd want to photograph graffiti. These two people have little or no interest in art but are nature enthusiasts. Thus, it's easy to comprehend their proclivity towards anything that represents natural landscapes.

Among my acquaintances who appear to be art aficionados, there's range in their response to art. There are those who keep up-to-date with art by visiting museums, reading and talking about it. Then there are those who are ignorant about art but don't want to show their ignorance and thus buy into anything that is classified as "art."

Then, there are the artists. I have artist friends who are just as closed-minded as my non-artist friends. That is, many of them can only see from their own point of view and see others' works as less important or valuable. Then there are those who either have no critical thinking ability or refuse to use it by accepting all art on its own terms. Of course, many fall somewhere in between this extreme range of thought.

As an art student, I met artists who create abstract works because they are bored with realism or because they are trying to find an expression of something that realism can't portray, or because they don't have the skills for drawing. I met landscape painters who love nature. I also met landscape painters who chose landscapes as their subject because they can't draw. As someone with good drawing skills, it was initially difficult for me to accept artists who cannot draw (this theme resonated with me when I saw it presented in the movie "Art School Confidential"). Most of the artists I admire, like Dali, Picasso, Matisse, Magritte, displayed a wide range of artistic accomplishments. Their drawing ability was a fundamental skill in their repertoire.

I learned about Rothko, an abstract expressionist whose work has no obvious reference to the real world. Yet, I met people who are insanely passionate about Rothko. Of course, there are others who think that appreciation of his artwork is a result of aggressive marketing. Who is right? Who is wrong? Is there a right or wrong in the world of art?

Is art appreciation simply an extension of the personality of the viewer? Can it be learned? Based on my experience, I'd say yes to both. I think that untutored minds appreciate art as an extension of their own personalities but appreciation can also be learned. The danger of being tutored, however, is that of becoming a victim of the psychology of "The Emperor's New Clothes".

The line between genuine, learned, and blind appreciation is blurry and fragile. I suppose that's why it's "art" and not "science".

We don't see things as they are, we see them as we are.

Anaïs Nin

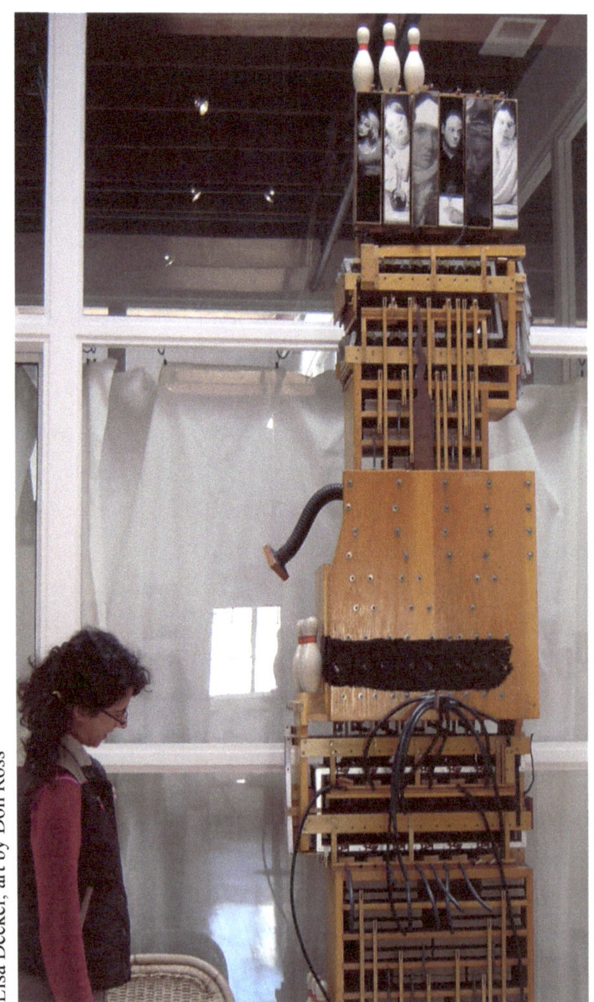

Lisa Decker, art by Don Ross

Epilogue: What is Art?

Art is a step from what is obvious and well-known toward what is arcane and concealed.

Khalil Gibran

"What is art?" is the question which initiated my journey through the visual narratives of the Mission. Instead of one answer, I discovered many different ways to view art and many stories along the way.

Now, a simple line of graffiti can excite me as much as a complicated piece by Rene Magritte; using my camera to capture the composition of a dead pigeon on the sidewalk can be as thrilling as photographing the angles of a Frank Gehry building.

This journey has taught me to "see" art instead of attempting to quantify it. I hope the images and stories in this book spark your imagination and inspire your creative explorations.

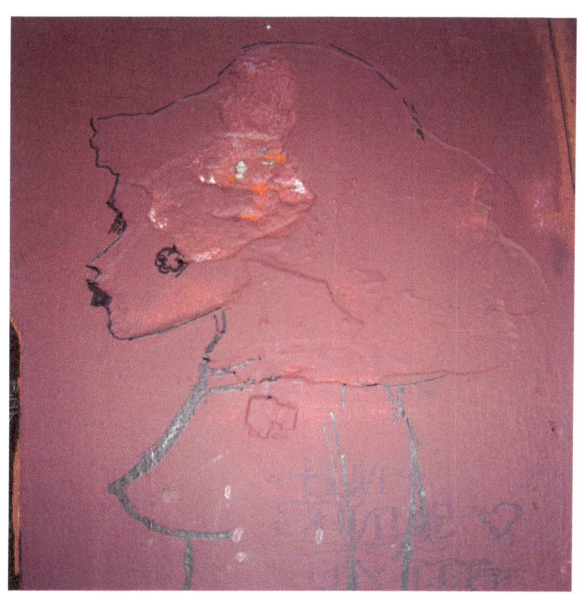

about the author

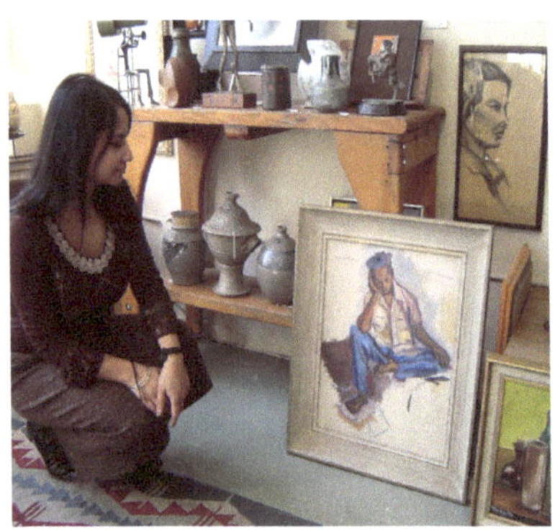

Leena Prasad lives and writes in the Mission-Dolores neighborhood of San Francisco. She writes a neuroscience column *Whose Brain Is It?* for synchchaos.com magazine and a music blog at InfiniteNotes.com.

She has written for public radio KQED's Spark website, Mission Arts Monthly magazine, India Currents magazine, and more. Please visit FishRidingABike.com for her writing portfolio.

She has a Journalism M.A. from Stanford University and published the South Asian literary magazine, Accent, prior to attending Stanford. At Stanford, she was a staff writer for the Stanford Daily.

When Leena is not writing, she puts her Computer Science B.S. from Tulane University to use in the Silicon Valley software industry and for developing fun websites which you can check out by starting at her homesite LeenaPrasad.com.

 leena@itfeltlikeakiss.com

 iTfeltLikeAkiss.com

 @iTfeltLikeAkiss

 iT felt Like A kiss (group)

www.ingramcontent.com/pod-product-compliance
Lightning Source LLC
LaVergne TN
LVHW070152110826
845147LV00002B/385

* 9 7 8 0 9 8 2 9 2 8 5 0 9 *